With the British Army in the Holy Land

With the British Army in the Holy Land

A Concise History of the Palestine Campaign
During the First World War

Henry Osmond Lock

LEONAUR

With the British Army in the Holy Land
A Concise History of the Palestine Campaign During the First World War
by Henry Osmond Lock

First published under the title
With the British Army in the Holy Land

Leonaur is an imprint of Oakpast Ltd

Copyright in this form © 2012 Oakpast Ltd

ISBN: 978-0-85706-928-3 (hardcover)
ISBN: 978-0-85706-929-0 (softcover)

http://www.leonaur.com

Publisher's Notes

Contents

Note

My aim in compiling this little book has been to provide a short account of the Palestine campaign, illustrated from the experiences of one who was present.

The manuscript was written on active service, soon after the occurrence of the events recorded. It may, on this account, be sketchy, but, it is hoped, not the less interesting.

My acknowledgments are due to the Official Despatches and publications, and also to the writings of Mr. W. T. Massey,[1] Official Correspondent with the Egyptian Expeditionary Force.

H. O. L.

In the Field, 1918.

---

1. *The Great War in the Middle East: the Desert Campaigns & How Jerusalem Was Won* and *The Great War in the Middle East: Allenby's Final Triumph* both by W. T. Massey are also published by Leonaur.

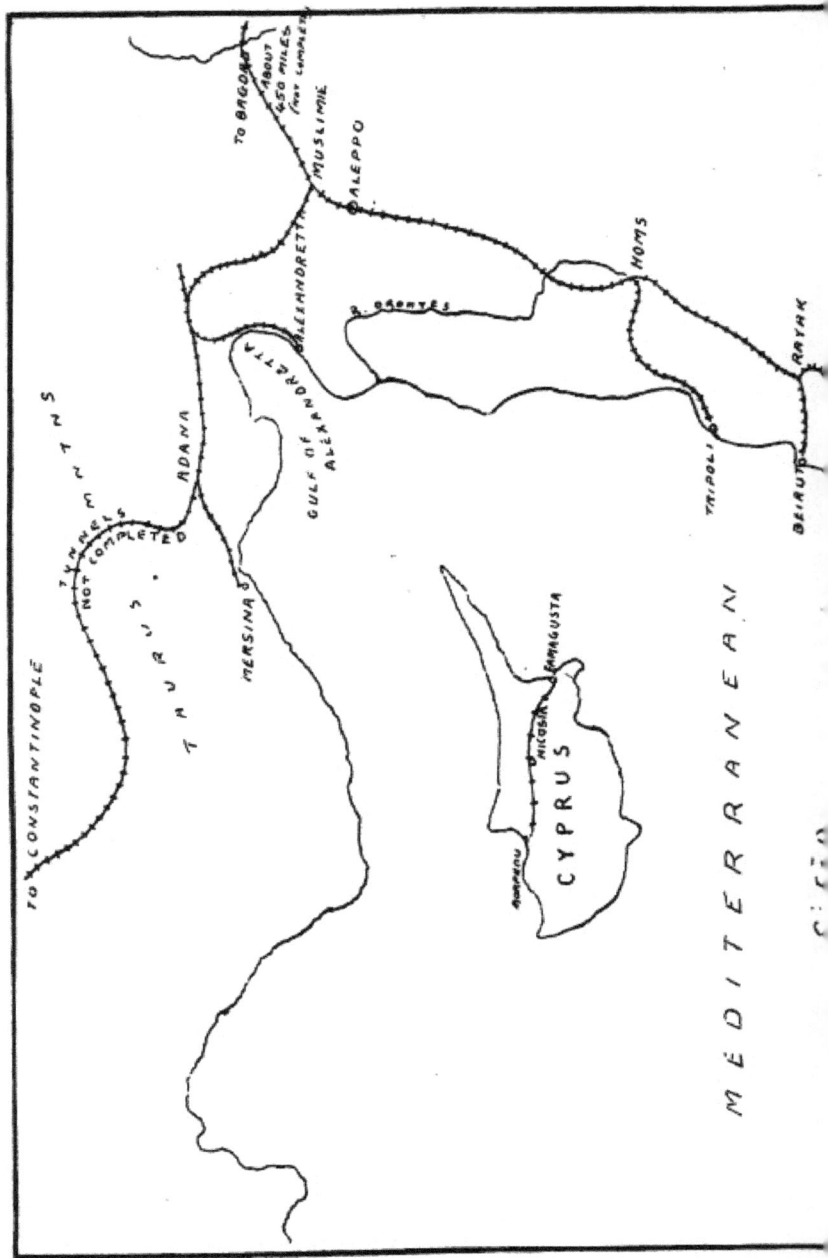

SKETCH MAP

SHOWING RAILWAYS IN 1914

Broad Gauge
Narrow Do

0   50   100
MILES

DAMASCUS
DERAA
SEA OF GALILEE
S Y R I A
Saviour's
HAIFA
JERUSALEM
DEAD SEA
JAFFA
BEERSHEBA
GAZA
RAFA
MAAN
FRONTIER
AKABA
GULF OF AKABA
S I N A I
PORT SAID
KANTARA
SUEZ CANAL
ISMAILIA
LAKES
NILE
E G Y P T
CAIRO
SUEZ
GULF OF SUEZ

CHAPTER 1

Egypt and the Suez Canal

The Holy Land has been the scene of war since the dawn of history. Long before Belgium became the cock-pit of Europe, Palestine was the cock-pit of the known world. Here, on the high road between Asia and Africa, were fought the great wars of Egyptians and Assyrians, Israelites and Canaanites, Greeks and Romans, Saracens and Crusaders. With these few square miles are associated the names of the world's greatest soldiers no less than that of the Prince of Peace. None can fail to be interested in the latest campaign in this Land of Armageddon.

To understand the causes and events that led up to the campaign in Palestine of 1917-1918, we must first summarize, as shortly as possible, the modern history of Egypt. That country had for many centuries formed an integral part of the Turkish Empire. But she had been rapidly slipping from the grasp of the Turk. Early in the nineteenth century Mohamed Ali had effectually thrown off the Turkish yoke. True, the Turkish suzerainty remained; but that authority was little more than nominal and was represented by an annual money tribute paid to the Porte by the Khedive out of the revenues of Egypt.

Both France and England had large financial interests in Egypt, especially after the construction of the Suez Canal, which was opened for traffic in 1869.

The Suez Canal, in fact, became of vital importance to Great Britain. By a stroke of policy the British Government acquired the shares of the almost bankrupt Khedive, Ismail Pasha, and thus had a holding in the company worth several million pounds. But far more important to Britain was the position of the Canal as the great artery of the British Empire, the most vulnerable point on the short sea route to India. Thus Britain became directly concerned in the affairs of Egypt, in its internal administration to secure peace within, and in its military defence to secure the country in general, and the Canal zone in particular, from invasion by a foreign enemy.

But the affairs of Egypt were in a most unsatisfactory condition. The army was wholly unreliable, and extravagance in high places had brought the exchequer to the verge of bankruptcy. In 1882 matters reached a crisis. A revolution broke out, headed by Arabi Pasha, and the situation looked desperate. Joint naval and military action by Britain and France was proposed, but the French ships sailed away and left Britain with a free hand. The British fleet bombarded the Forts at Alexandria and a military force, based on the Suez Canal, was landed at Ismailia. This force completely defeated the army of Arabi Pasha at Tel-el-Kebir, put down the rebellion, and restored the government of the then Khedive, Tewfik Pasha. But the Khedivial Government had been unable to cope with the rebellion single-handed; it had only been restored to power by British arms; it could not hope to retain that power unless continuously backed by the power of Britain.

From this time forward, whether she liked it or not, Britain found herself effectually saddled with the direction of the government of Egypt. In this position she became more fully confirmed by the Anglo-Egyptian military operations against the Soudan in 1885, under Gordon, and in 1898, under Kitchener. Outstanding differences with France were dispelled on the conclusion of the Anglo-French Entente Cordiale, and Britain was left virtually mistress of Egypt.

Let us look for a minute at the military geography of Egypt, particularly with regard to the security of her frontiers from invasion. Egypt consists, or prior to the seventies consisted, of the Nile, its valley and delta, and the country rendered fertile by that river. On either side of this fertile belt is dry, barren desert. On the north is the Mediterranean Sea, and on the south the tropical Soudan. Thus, in the hands of a power that holds the command of the sea, Egypt is well adapted for defence. The tropical Soudan makes a well-nigh impossible line of advance for a large hostile force from the south, and the routes of approach from the east and from the west, across the waterless deserts, present obstacles scarcely less formidable.

Since the seventies, however, another important factor has entered the problem, namely, the Suez Canal and the area of cultivation and civilization which has sprung up along its banks. The large amount of fresh water required for the maintenance of the Canal, for the use of the towns that have sprung up along its banks, and for the existence of the large population which the Canal has attracted, is brought by a Canal known as the Sweet Water Canal, from the river Nile. This Sweet Water Canal, and the piped services which it supplied, were, in 1914, wholly upon the western or Egyptian side of the Suez Canal. This western side was also well provided with communications. Trunk railways connected Ismailia, at the centre of the Canal, with Cairo and Alexandria, and lateral railways, running along the whole length of the Canal, connected it with Port Said and Suez.

Although, as was subsequently discovered, the problem of defending the Suez Canal was by no means the same as that of defending Egypt, the problems may, at first sight, appear identical. An enemy force moving from Palestine against the Suez Canal and Egypt, would have to cross a comparatively waterless desert for a distance of over a hundred miles. On coming into collision with the defenders of the Canal, such an enemy would be operating far from his base, with a long and vulnerable line of communications, and with little or no available fresh water. The defenders, operating along the line of the Suez Canal, would be close to their base, with admirable communications, both lateral and to the rear, and with the rich cultivated lands of Egypt on which to draw for supplies, whilst their supply of fresh water would be unlimited.

The boundary line between Egypt and Palestine in 1914 ran from Rafa, on the Mediterranean, to the head of the Gulf of Akaba, the north-eastern arm of the Red Sea. This line runs right across the desert and is distant about 120 miles from the Suez Canal. At first sight the boundary seems ideal, and in so far as the defence of Egypt alone was concerned, it left little or nothing to be desired. But, as subsequent events proved, this line was not good enough to safeguard the defences of the Canal.

On the outbreak of war, in August, 1914, between Germany and Austria-Hungary on the one hand, and Great Britain, France, Russia and Belgium on the other, the garrison of Egypt was augmented by troops sent out from England and India and from Australia. The Suez Canal, through which vast numbers of troops were passing, was of vital importance to the communications of the allies, and was strongly guarded accordingly. Two months later (November 5), Turkey threw in her hand with the Central Powers. One of the baits held out by Germany to induce the Turks to enter the struggle, was a promise that they should be restored to complete supremacy in Egypt. With the entering of Turkey into the war, and her open threats to invade Egypt, the protection of that country and of the Canal became a matter of extreme urgency.

The policy of defence adopted was that of making the line of the Canal the line of resistance. A large portion of the low-lying desert to the north-east of the Canal was flooded, so as to render approach by that direction impossible. Warships took up stations in the Canal itself, while naval patrol launches took over the duty of guarding the Bitter Lakes. The troops detailed for the defence of the Canal itself were entrenched upon the western side, with reserves concentrated at points of tactical importance. In this way full advantage was taken of the lateral communications on the western side of the Canal, while it was thought that the difficulties of crossing the desert on the eastern side would make approach by the Turks well-nigh impossible.

Meanwhile, the Turk was not letting the grass grow under his feet. Whether the Germans ever intended to pay the price for Turkish adhesion by sending a strong enough force to make the invasion of Egypt practicable is open to doubt. The Turkish rank and file were certainly led to believe that a serious invasion of Egypt was intended. But it is much more likely that the object of the Germans was to detain as large a British force as possible in Egypt and thus prevent their taking part in the fighting in France. A secondary object may have been to render the Suez Canal temporarily impassable. Whatever may have been the chestnuts that Germany hoped to get out of the fire, it was clear that Turkey was willing to act as catspaw, and attempt a foolhardy invasion of Egypt.

Consequently, the construction of a new military railway in Syria was put in hand, and by January, 1915, the Turks had formed advanced posts at Auja, on the frontier, and also at Kosseima, El Arish, and Khan Epenus in the desert. The problem of water supply has always presented a difficulty to armies crossing this waterless desert. There are a certain number of reservoirs and cisterns which hold up water during the rains. In the winter time these would be full. The Turk is less particular about the water which he drinks than the white man, and doubtless he could, to some extent, be supplied from some of the brackish pools in the desert, with water that no one would think of offering to a British soldier.

The light pontoons that the Turks dragged across the desert for crossing the Canal are said to have been used for carrying water during certain stages of the advance. Suffice it to say that the Turks did succeed in solving the water problem, and in crossing the desert with a force of some considerable strength.

On the 3rd February, 1915, the threatened attack materialized. Before dawn, some of the light pontoons which the Turks had brought with them, were launched on the Canal. These were manned, while other Turks deployed along the eastern bank and opened fire to cover the crossing. The troops defending this portion of the Canal, mostly Indians, opened fire upon the pontoons, with the result that many of them were sunk. Two of the pontoons, however, reached the western bank, and their crews, numbering about twenty, surrendered. There was fighting throughout the day, but no further crossing of the Canal. On the next day the east bank was swept, with the result that a considerable party of the enemy were captured. After this, the Turks withdrew, and marched back to Palestine. This was the only time that a formed body of the enemy succeeded in reaching the Canal. But they had shown that it was possible for them to achieve the almost impossible, and thus they gave the authorities responsible for the defence of Egypt much food for thought.

The menace to Egypt was for a time delayed, though not wholly removed, by the expedition against the Dardanelles.

To co-operate with our Russian allies, the British Government decided, early in 1915, to attempt to force the passage of the Dardanelles. The strategic gains promised were highly attractive, and included—the passage of arms and munitions from the allies to Russia in exchange for wheat, the neutrality and possible adherence of the outstanding Balkan States, the severing of communications between European and Asiatic Turkey, the drawing off of Turkish troops from the theatres of the war, and the expulsion of the Turks from Constantinople, and ultimately from Europe. Incidentally, it was considered, on the principle that the best defensive is an offensive, that a thrust at the very heart of Turkey, a threat against Constantinople itself, would afford the best means of defending Egypt.

The story of the Dardanelles expedition has been often told, and scarcely forms a part of this history, so a few words must suffice. In February, 1915, we started by bombarding the forts with a few old warships. The forts at the outer entrance were soon silenced, and early in March, the warships moved up to the Narrows. On the 18th, a great effort was made to reduce the forts about the Narrows; but it failed, with the loss of three battleships and more than 2,000 men. This demonstrated the fact that the Dardanelles could never be opened by sea power alone, and, accordingly, amphibious operations became necessary. An expeditionary force was assembled in Egypt, and Mudros was selected as the advanced base. On April 25, landings were effected on the extreme point of the Gallipoli Peninsula. In spite of heroic attempts, we did little more than effect a precarious lodgement. Further operations were necessary; additional divisions were brought out from home; and on the night of the 6th/7th August, another landing was effected at Suvla Bay.

But the new plan was no more successful than the old. Within a couple of days this force also had settled down to a war of positions. Winter was approaching; our positions on the peninsula would then become no longer tenable. No progress could be made, and at length it was decided to evacuate. The Suvla Bay force was withdrawn first; and the evacuation of the main body of troops was completed on the 20th December. The withdrawal was carried out with the same brilliance that had characterized the various landings, and with so small a number of casualties that it was described as "an achievement without parallel in the annals of war."

Many of the regiments that fought against the Turks at Gallipoli were withdrawn, directly or indirectly to Egypt, and subsequently met the Turk again during the advance into Palestine. Included among these were the 10th, 52nd, 53rd and 54th Divisions, besides regiments of Anzacs and Yeomanry. In so far as the Dardanelles operations aimed at protecting Egypt, they were a success; for, while they were in progress, no organized invasion of Egypt was attempted. But the evacuation had the effect of liberating a large force of Turkey's best troops for operations against Mesopotamia and Egypt.

It would be convenient to pause here and take stock of the military situation in Egypt, in the light of over a year's experience of actual war.

In the first place, the Turks had disillusioned us as to the impossibility of crossing the waterless desert, and had actually crossed it with a considerable armed and organized force. They announced that what they had effected had been nothing more than a reconnaissance. In any case, they had shown us what they could do, and that, backed by the resources of the Central Powers, there would be no insuperable obstacle to their bringing a large and fully equipped army across the desert.

In the second place, we had discovered that the problems of defending the Suez Canal and of defending Egypt were not identical. While the Canal formed an admirable moat, an obstacle difficult to negotiate when stoutly defended, and so a capital defensive line for the protection of the Nile; yet this line was inadequate for the protection of the Canal itself or for securing the immunity of the passing shipping.

And so, thirdly, we realized that some other line must be found for the protection of the Canal. While we were sitting on the west bank, small parties of Turks approached the eastern bank. On more than one occasion, in the summer of 1915, they succeeded in placing mines in the fairway of the Canal. It would, therefore, have been quite possible for them to have seriously interfered with the working of the Canal and the passage of shipping. Granted that a new line must be found, the question arises where such new line should be drawn. A line across the actual desert may be all very well in war time, though none too easy to hold, for the reasons that we have already discussed. But to keep a garrison on such a line for ever would be well-nigh intolerable. Thus, by a process of elimination, we find that the most suitable line for the permanent defence of the Suez Canal is the fertile country beyond the eastern desert—in other words, Palestine.

Fourthly, it had been brought home to us that the worst form of defence is a passive defence. As, therefore, the Turk would not leave well alone, but insisted on attacking us in Egypt, so it became necessary for us to meet him on his own ground, to push a vigorous offensive, and eventually to carry the war into Palestine.

CHAPTER 2

The Desert of Sinai

In accordance with the policy of defending the Suez Canal upon a line further east, the construction of a new defensive line was put in hand during the early months of 1916. No longer were the Turks to be allowed to annoy us by actually reaching the Canal. A line of trenches, protected by barbed wire entanglements, was constructed out in the desert, a few miles to the east of the Canal. As may be imagined, this was no easy task. A large amount of excavation was necessary for a small amount of trench; walls had to be built up with sandbags; and other steps had to be taken to prevent the sides from foundering, and to construct a work that would withstand shell fire.

Meanwhile, other preparations were put in hand for carrying the defensive line further to the east. The construction was commenced of a broad gauge of railway from Kantara eastwards across the desert. This railway eventually became the trunk line between Egypt and Palestine. In the days of trench warfare before Gaza, it transported freight trains heavily laden with rations and ammunitions, troop trains conveying officers and men in open trucks, hospital trains evacuating sick and wounded, and an all-sleeping-car express running nightly in each direction. In 1918, a swing-bridge was improvised across the Suez Canal, and Jerusalem and Cairo were then connected by rail without change of carriage being necessary. The future prospects of this railway seem unbounded.

It will undoubtedly be continued through to Damascus and Aleppo, where it will connect with railways to Constantinople and to Baghdad and the Persian Gulf. Thus it will form part of a grand trunk railway system along the old caravan routes connecting the three continents of Europe, Asia, and Africa. In its conception, it was just a military railway, laid, with but little preparation, across the sands of the desert.

To this railway, however, was largely due the success of the campaign that we are about to consider.

We have already seen that the Sinaitic Desert is almost waterless. Although it has often been crossed by invading armies in both directions, the provision of water has always presented the greatest difficulty. The carriage of water in tanks upon the backs of camels, a method used by us for locally supplying troops between water dumps and the headquarters of units, proved successful here thousands of years ago. The plan adopted by the Turks of dragging water-holding pontoons across the desert was not to be despised. Further progress was made when supplies of water were transported in tank-trucks along the railway. But a bolder adaptation of modern science to desert fighting was reached, when it was decided to lay on a piped supply of water from the Nile.

We have seen that the western bank of the Suez Canal was already provided with a plentiful supply of fresh water by the Sweet Water Canal. Plant was now installed for making this water available for the troops. Purity had to be considered as well as adequacy of supply. A peculiar danger had to be guarded against. There is a disease prevalent in Egypt, of a particularly unpleasant character and persistent type, called by the medical profession Bilhaziosis, but better known to our men as "Bill Harris." This disease is conveyed by a parasitic worm found in the waters of the Nile, and affects not only those who drink the water, but also those who bathe in it or merely wash. Consequently, orders were stringent against even touching Nile water which had not previously been treated. This necessitated the troops east of the Canal being put upon a very restricted supply, and they were accordingly rationed at the rate of a gallon of water per head per day for all purposes, including washing, cooking and drinking.

At the Kantara waterworks water was drawn in from the Sweet Water Canal, mixed with alum, and pumped through settling tanks into filters. When it had passed through these, it was pumped underneath the Suez Canal into reservoirs on the eastern bank. Here it was chlorinated; and hence the water, now fit for all purposes, was pumped forward to its destination. There being no gradient to assist the natural flow of the water, it had to be pumped forward by successive stages. The first stage was as far as Romani; when working at greatest length the pumping stages numbered no less than seventeen. At times, during the advance, the railway had to be called in aid; and train-loads of water for the use of advanced troops were railed from pipe-head up to rail-head.

At some stages of the advance this supply could be supplemented by local water, which, though generally somewhat brackish, was employed for the horses, mules and camels. It was even found to have no ill-effect upon the troops, if used for a limited period, and if necessary precautions were taken. At other stages, where water was non-existent, or rendered wholly unapproachable by enemy dispositions, our force became entirely dependent upon the supply delivered through the pipe-line. Ultimately, when we settled down to protracted trench warfare before Gaza, this pipe-line was delivering a constant supply of water into our trenches, distant some couple of hundred miles from the banks of the Nile.

Kantara started upon a process of development worthy of the base of such an expedition. Before the war, it had been little more than a small Canal village, comprising a few huts. It eventually grew into an important railway terminus with wharves and cranes, a railway ferry and 40 miles of sidings. Miles of first-class macadamized roads were made, vast ordnance and supply dumps arose, and camps and depots were established for man and beast. The scale on which this mushroom town developed was stupendous.

Early in 1916, the Turks, relieved from imminent danger near home by our evacuation of Gallipoli, came down again in force through Syria, Palestine and the desert, to attack us in Egypt. Our construction gangs, engaged upon the new railway and upon the development of local water supplies, were at this time covered by escorts, mainly of cavalry, spread out upon a wide front. On the 23rd of April several thousand Turks, operating in three columns, attacked our desert posts at Oghratina, Katia and Dueidar respectively, the two former being about 30 miles and the last named about 10 miles to the east of Kantara. Oghratina and Katia, being well out in the desert, were cavalry posts held by yeomanry.

These two posts were rushed by a large force of the enemy under cover of fog, and, though a stubborn resistance was offered, and the fighting was severe, the posts were overwhelmed. At Dueidar, an infantry post, some 20 miles or so nearer our base, the Turk was less successful. Under cover of the same fog, about 900 Turks tried to rush this post at dawn. They found the garrison standing to, and were beaten off. Though they made three distinct attempts to break through, they were unsuccessful. The garrison was reinforced and the Turks were repulsed.

In order to hamper or prevent such bodies of Turks from again crossing the desert and approaching the Canal, it was decided to draw off the local water supplies in the desert. Accordingly, these supplies, mainly in pools and cisterns constructed by men in a bygone age, were systematically pumped or drained dry. By the end of June, no water was left available for enemy use within easy reach of the Canal. From this time forward the enemy attempted no more sporadic raids. He concentrated instead upon a serious attack against our main positions, which attack materialized at Romani.

By July, 1916, our railway had reached the village of Romani, which is some 25 miles from Kantara, and is in the neighbourhood of Oghratina and Katia, where the enemy had secured his success in April. The Turkish force had been stiffened with Germans and Austrians, and was under the command of the German General Von Kressenstein. It moved from the Turkish railroad at Auja on the frontier, and advanced by way of Maghdaba and the Wadi El Arish to El Arish, and thence westward along the caravan route towards Egypt. This force had been well equipped and trained for this class of warfare, and it succeeded in dragging heavy guns across the desert byroads which it improvised for the purpose. Making his advanced base at Bir-el-Abd, the enemy first occupied and fortified a line about Mageiba.

On the morning of the 3rd August, he made a general advance, and took up a line fronting our position at Romani. Here our left flank rested on the sea; the left of the line was held by the 52nd Division, while the 53rd Division was on the right. The East Lancashire Division was in reserve. The right flank comprised a chain of posts, behind which were a force of cavalry. The weak point was, therefore, our right flank, for a little force working round by the south would threaten our communications and might possibly cut us off from our reinforcements down the line and from our base at Kantara. Accordingly, on the night of the 3rd/4th, one Light Horse Brigade moved out to hold a three-miles line from our infantry post on the right, sending out patrols a considerable distance in front.

About midnight, the enemy were found to be advancing in this direction. Before light next morning this brigade were heavily engaged, holding up the advance of a considerable body of the enemy. Gradually the brigade were pressed back by weight of numbers, until, at about five o'clock in the morning, the timely arrival of reinforcements secured the complete arrest of the enemy advance in this direction. Soon after daylight the enemy swung round his left flank and established himself upon Mount Royston. This enforced upon us a further retirement; but he had reached the limit of his success. Towards the sea, the enemy attacks against the 52nd Division were beaten off, and here he could make no progress.

At about 5.30 in the afternoon, a counter-attack was launched against Mount Royston, and this position was recaptured. Early on the following morning, the 5th, before daylight, the 52nd Division recaptured Wellington Ridge, the last of our lost positions remaining in the hands of the Turk. The tide had now turned definitely in our favour and the Turk was in full retreat. An attempt was made to encircle his southern flank and to cut him off with our cavalry, but his rearguard actions were fought stubbornly, and the pursuing cavalry had to be withdrawn. During the night of the 5th/6th, the enemy evacuated Katia, which was occupied by us on the following morning. By the 8th, he had abandoned Oghratina, and had fallen back to his advanced base at Bir-el-Abd. From this base he now proceeded to evacuate camps and stores, but he was not allowed to do so unmolested. He was followed up by the whole of our cavalry and effectually shelled by our horse artillery.

On the afternoon and evening of this day (the 8th) the Turk counter-attacked our cavalry, who were clearly outnumbered. Nevertheless the Turk considered it more prudent to burn the remainder of his stores. He completed the evacuation of Abd by the 12th, and it remained in our hands from this time forward. This abortive advance against Romani marked the last determined attempt of the Turks to invade the Suez Canal and Egypt. Henceforth the efforts of the Turks were confined to opposing the storm which their misguided cupidity had raised up against them.

After the battle of Romani, our mounted troops held a line about Abd. The enemy now consolidated a position at Mazar, a little more than 20 miles further to the east. In the middle of September, a cavalry column moved out to Mazar and attacked the Turkish positions. Neither side was anxious to bring on a general engagement at that time. However, the losses which the Turk suffered in this operation caused him sufficient uneasiness to induce him to withdraw altogether from Mazar. He therefore withdrew his troops to a position close to El Arish.

The Turkish garrison at El Arish consisted of some 1,600 infantry in all, in a strong entrenched position. In the second week of December increased activity was shown by the Turks, and aerial reconnaissance of their camps behind their front line showed evidence of the proximity of reinforcements. Our preparations for a forward move were pressed on strenuously, and, though they were somewhat delayed through lack of water, we were ready to move by the 20th December.

The enemy realized that the swiftness of our final preparations had been too much for him. Knowing that his reinforcements could not arrive in time, he hurriedly withdrew his troops from El Arish. This retirement was reported by the R.F.C. on the 20th December, and our mounted troops, supported by infantry, were ordered to move on El Arish the same night. The town was found to be evacuated. Aircraft reports showed that about 1,600 of the enemy were on the march, in two columns, in the neighbourhood of Maghdaba and Abu Aweigila, while Sheikh Zowaid and Rafa appeared to be clear. The enemy were evidently not retreating by the caravan route towards Gaza, but were falling back southwards by the Wadi El Arish (the Biblical "River of Egypt") upon their rail-head at Auja.

This evidence went to show that the garrison which had recently evacuated El Arish were at Maghdaba, and it seemed likely that this force were preparing to hold Maghdaba as a rearguard. A flying column of cavalry was immediately despatched against them from El Arish. This column found the enemy strongly posted and entrenched on both banks of the Wadi El Arish. An attack was set in motion on the morning of the 23rd December, and lasted for the greater part of the day. By half-past four that afternoon, however, all organized resistance was over, and the enemy were surrendering everywhere. No further advance was attempted along the enemy's line of communications towards Auja, and the troops, being but a flying column, retired at once to El Arish.

Within a few days after the destruction at Maghdaba of the rearguard, or garrison withdrawing from El Arish, another body of the enemy started to entrench a position at Magruntein near Rafa. This was obviously intended to bar our progress eastwards along the coastal route, the old caravan route to Gaza. Rafa is the frontier town upon the Turco-Egyptian frontier. The operation to which we are about to refer was, therefore, the last engagement that took place upon Egyptian territory. It was not possible at the end of December for the British force to push on and occupy Rafa permanently, owing to difficulties of supply. But since the enemy had again placed a small detached garrison within striking distance of our mounted troops, the temptation was held out for a repetition of the Maghdaba success at

Magruntein.

Accordingly, a flying column, composed wholly of mounted troops and artillery, moved out from El Arish on the evening of the 8th/9th January, 1917. The enemy was taken completely by surprise, and by dawn on the 9th January his position was almost entirely surrounded. The position, however, was a formidable one, with ground in front entirely open and devoid of cover. The main attack was timed for ten o'clock a.m., and was delivered from the east and south-east. The town of Rafa was soon occupied, and, in the course of the morning, our attack against the Turkish system of defences developed on every side. The enemy's works were dominated by a central redoubt or keep, and orders were given for a concerted attack to be developed against this at 3.30 p.m. Meanwhile the enemy had despatched a relieving force from Shellal, which is about twenty miles to the south-east of Rafa and mid-way between that town and the nearest Turkish railway. This relieving force was detected by our aircraft, who frequently attacked it with bombs and machine gun fire.

Orders were at once given for the attack on the redoubt to be pressed with vigour, and, before five o'clock, the redoubt was captured. With this position in our hands, the remaining works soon fell, and by 5.30 p.m. all organized resistance was over, and the enemy position, with all its garrison, was captured. The relieving force were driven off without much difficulty, and withdrew, presumably, to Shellal, which thereafter became the enemy's next point of concentration. Our column, taking with them all prisoners, animals and captured material, withdrew again to El Arish.

From the time of our occupation of El Arish on the 22nd December, that town developed apace. Mine-sweeping operations were at once commenced in the roadstead, a pier was erected, and, on the 24th, the supply ships from Port Said began unloading stores and supplies. The lie of the land gives unlimited opportunity to a power having the command of the sea to supplement his other means of bringing forward supplies by landing sea-borne goods upon the open beach. Repeatedly, in the subsequent history of this war, we availed ourselves of this means of supply, as our army moved northwards in Palestine.

The landing of stores at El Arish, however, was not wholly successful, owing to the strong currents, a shelving and shifting beach, and heavy surf. In winter, the sea is apt to be stormy here, and then such landing may become impossible. Supplies were also hastened to El Arish by camel convoy, and dumps were accumulated. The railway was pushed on with and, before the end of January, the railway station at El Arish was completed; during the following month the railway was pushed further out along the coast preparatory to another advance.

After the destruction of their post at Rafa, the Turks immediately began to concentrate their forces near Shellal. West of this place they prepared a strong defensive position near Wali Sheikh Nuran, with the object of covering their lines of communication both along the Beersheba railway and along the Jerusalem-Hebron-Beersheba road. They also established themselves at Khan Yunus, on the coastal road a few miles to the east of Rafa. On the 23rd February, a reconnaissance was carried out against Khan Yunus. The column, arriving at dawn, found the position strongly held, and, after manoeuvring the enemy out of his front line of defence and capturing prisoners, withdrew without difficulty. Continuous pressure maintained by our troops in this neighbourhood, however, induced the enemy to withdraw the garrison of Khan Yunus, which place was entered by our cavalry without opposition on the 28th February. The enemy also evacuated without firing a shot the position which he had prepared near Wali Sheikh Nuran.

Our troops had crossed the desert with success attending them at every stage. And now at last they had set foot in the Promised Land. Many of them must have felt, what a soldier was afterwards heard to express, "This may be the land of promise; it's certainly not the land of fulfilment." History repeats itself. As the Israelites had much trial and suffering to endure after reaching this stage of their journey from Egypt, before they were permitted to "go in and possess the land," so had our lads many a fierce and bloody battle to fight before they, too, might set foot within the Holy City.

A few words as to personnel may not be out of place before we leave the subject of this desert campaign. Throughout this time the commander-in-chief of the Egyptian Expeditionary Force was General Sir Archibald Murray, G.C.M.G., K.C.B. A reorganization of the force took place in October, 1917, in consequence of which General Murray moved his headquarters back from Ismailia to Cairo. At the same time, the new headquarters of the Eastern Force came into existence at Ismailia under the command of Lieut.-General Sir Charles Dobell, K.C.B., C.M.G., D.S.O., under whose direction thus came more immediately the operations in the eastern desert.

Amongst the troops employed were the Australians and New Zealanders and several regiments of English Yeomanry, and, included among the infantry, were the 52nd (Lowland), the 53rd (Welsh and Home Counties), the 54th (East Anglian) and the 74th (Dismounted Yeomanry) Divisions.

This review of the advance across the desert has of necessity been superficial. Strictly speaking, the desert campaign is outside the scope of this book. But a summarized history of the advance forms a necessary introduction to our subject. Here, on the threshold of Palestine, we must leave this army for a short space, while we review some other operations, and while we take a glance at the nature of the country in which this army was about to operate.

CHAPTER 3

Mesopotamia, the Caucasus, and the Hejaz

Having taken a hurried glance at the campaign in Sinai, which directly led up to that in Palestine, we will take a yet more hurried glance at three other campaigns in Asiatic Turkey which had their bearing, direct or indirect, upon the Palestine operations.

Most important among these was the expedition to Mesopotamia. In 1914, when Turkey came into the war against us, a British Indian Brigade was landed at the mouth of the Shatt-el-Arab, the common estuary by which the Tigris and the Euphrates reach the Persian Gulf. The objects of this expedition were to secure the oil-fields of Persia in which Britain was largely interested; to neutralize German ascendancy, which was rapidly developing in this part of the world through her interests in the Baghdad Railway; and to embarrass Turkey by attacking her at a point where facilities of manoeuvre and supply seemed to hold out a reasonable promise of success.

Throughout 1915 this expedition met with uninterrupted success. The British Indian forces engaged were increased in number and strength, and, in spite of appalling conditions of climate, and notwithstanding more than one narrow escape from disaster, the British flag was pushed further and further forward into this flat alluvial country. In the autumn of 1915, we held all the country up to Nasiriyeh on the Euphrates and to Kut el Amara on the Tigris. Then that ill-fated decision was arrived at which sent General Townshend, with the inadequate force at his command, up the Tigris to capture Baghdad. This force went heroically forward, and, just short of that city, defeated the Turks at the battle of Ctesiphon.

But General Townshend's casualties were heavy, and his available reinforcements were neither sufficiently numerous nor at hand. The pick of the Turkish Army released by our withdrawal from Gallipoli, had poured down to reinforce the enemy, and General Townshend had no alternative but to beat a hasty retreat. Accordingly, he fell back to Kut el Amara. Partly from inability to get his war-worn forces further away, and partly from a disinclination to abandon this important tactical point to the enemy, he consolidated here and prepared to withstand a siege.

The history of that siege will live as one of the noblest in the annals of the British Army. But the stars in their courses fought against us. Strong enemy positions, inadequate supplies and transport arrangements, floods, and appalling conditions of country and weather, proved overwhelming. In spite of the unremitting efforts of the relieving army, which fought battle after battle without stint of labour or loss, the garrison of Kut found themselves, at the beginning of May, 1916, left with no alternative but to capitulate. Almost the whole of the garrison were removed into Asia Minor, to a captivity which few were destined to survive. Naturally the Turks were much elated by this success, following upon their successes in Gallipoli, and were persuaded that the might of the British arm was nothing which they need fear.

Leaving a sufficient force to check any further British advance into Mesopotamia, the Turk withdrew the bulk of his forces to operate against the Russians and, perhaps wisely, made no great effort to dislodge us from the territory which we already occupied. The opposing forces sat down and watched each other for many months in the entrenched positions below Kut. In March of the following year, 1917, General Maude, on whom had fallen the command of the British Army in Mesopotamia, won a decisive victory at Kut; and, pursuing the remnants of the routed enemy, entered Baghdad. The Turks withdrew to the higher country north and north-east of the city, whither they were pursued.

After these operations, the British were in occupation of the completed section of the Baghdad railway, which was then open from Baghdad as far north as Samarra. They also effected a junction with the Russian troops operating in Persia. In the following September, engagements were fought at Ramadi and elsewhere on the Euphrates, with the result that the Turkish garrisons were rounded up, and but few Turkish troops were left to oppose the British forces in Mesopotamia. Nevertheless, an immediate advance was not made up to Mosul and the upper territories of Mesopotamia.

Owing to the collapse of Russia, it became necessary for us to take over some of the country in Persia, which had previously been occupied by Russian troops, and an expedition was also sent to assist the Armenians at Baku on the Caspian Sea. Other troops which could be spared from Mesopotamia were sent round, in the spring of 1918, to take part in the operations in Palestine, and the forces that remained were devoted to the garrisoning and consolidation of the territory already occupied.

A glance at the map of Turkey in Asia will show that the provinces of Mesopotamia and Syria consist of long narrow strips of fertile country bordered by desert, and resemble two legs which fork at Aleppo.

As far as Aleppo, troops and supplies from Europe passed over one common route. From the Turkish point of view, therefore, the campaigns in these two countries were to some extent interdependent. This enabled the Turks to concentrate a reserve at Aleppo, ready to be moved down into either theatre of war as the exigencies of the situation might demand. Conversely, therefore, a British offensive in Mesopotamia might draw off troops destined for Palestine, or an offensive in Palestine might attract troops otherwise intended for operations in Mesopotamia. There is strong evidence that a Turco-German offensive was contemplated in Mesopotamia for 1918.

In the spring of that year, however, a British offensive was undertaken in Palestine, which had the immediate effect of drawing to that country strong Turkish and German reinforcements from Aleppo. Nothing more was heard of the offensive in Mesopotamia, and, by the autumn of 1918, there was scarcely a fighting Turk to be found in that country. Just as our expedition against the Dardanelles, by engaging the enemy at a vital spot near home, had materially assisted the defence of Egypt, so did our offensives in Palestine materially assist the defence of Mesopotamia.

Turning to another corner of the map of Turkey, where Europe and Asia meet in the mountains of the Caucasus, we see that the Turkish frontier here marches with that of Russia. In the earlier days of the war, the Russians carried out an important and successful advance in this neighbourhood, and, early in 1916, occupied the cities of Trebizond and Erzerum. Thus, at the time when the campaign in Palestine was embarked upon, the armies of the allies were closing in upon Eastern Turkey simultaneously from three directions, the Russian Caucasus army from the north-east, the British Mesopotamian army from the south-east, and the Egyptian Expeditionary Force from the south. Strategically, the situation seemed full of promise.

But, in the winter of 1917-18, followed the disastrous collapse of Russia, and the setting free of many Turkish soldiers of good quality from all the Russian fronts for service elsewhere. We had hoped that our offensive in Syria might have been supported by the co-operation of the Russians. Instead, we felt the pinch of their defection in the stiffening of enemy resistance on our front by the transfer of good troops from the Caucasus to Palestine.

There is yet another theatre of warfare in Asiatic Turkey, the operations in which exerted considerable influence on those in Palestine. The whole of the eastern shores of the Red Sea formed part of the Ottoman Empire. The southernmost sector, known as the Yemen, was the farthest outpost of that Empire. Here a few Turks and Arabs conducted a sporadic warfare against our garrison at Aden, more calculated to cause annoyance and to detain a British force of some strength than to exercise much influence upon the war as a whole.

Farther to the north, on this Red Sea littoral, is a province of much more importance, the Hejaz, in which are situate the most holy of cities in the Moslem world, Mecca and Medina. To Christians, the Hejaz is forbidden ground. To Mahomedans, it is the focus of pilgrimage from all parts of the world. The Sultan of Turkey, as the ruler of Mecca, is looked up to by the Sunni or orthodox Mahomedans in all lands as the spiritual head of their Church. Though rulers of the Hejaz, the Turks were not at one with the local population. These are Arabs, and to them the Turkish rule was as unpopular as to most other non-Turkish subjects of that decaying Empire. Profiting by Turkey's embarrassments in other parts, the Arabs rose in the summer of 1916, resolved on ridding themselves of the hated Turkish yoke. Sheikh Hussein of Mecca was proclaimed King of the Hejaz.

At this time there were garrisons of Turkish troops stationed at Mecca, Medina and at the port of Jiddah. Their communication with Turkey was by the recently opened railway to Damascus and Aleppo. This railway, south of Damascus, ran along the high plateau on the eastern side of the Dead Sea, through Maan, and along the desert to Medina. The intention was to carry the line ultimately through to Mecca, but at this time it was only open for traffic as far as Medina. The revolt broke out on the 5th June, 1916, at which date a cordon was spread round Medina. Jiddah was attacked on the 9th, and capitulated after holding out for only a week. The bulk of the Mecca garrison were at this time at Taif. Accordingly, the town of Mecca passed into the hands of the *emir*, with the exception of the ports. These put up a small fight, but had all surrendered by the middle of July. The force at Taif were blockaded, and, on the 23rd September, this force also surrendered. By this time, all the outlying garrisons had been disposed of, and the Hejaz generally cleared of Turks.

Meanwhile, Medina had not only held out, but had been reinforced, and the fighting strength brought up to some 14,000. Late in September, the Turks sallied out and established a cordon of posts at a distance of some 30 to 40 miles from the city. They also pushed further afield; but, Arab armies moving up from the south, the Turks withdrew, at the end of the year, behind the cordon of posts which they had established. For the next six months, the railway to the north of Medina was frequently raided by the Arabs, but the town was effectually cut off from its communications with Turkey.

In July, 1917, Akaba, at the head of the gulf of that name, the north-eastern arm of the Red Sea, was captured. This is at no great distance from Maan, an important depot on the Hejaz Railway, the last outpost of Syria at the edge of the desert of North Arabia. From Akaba, the railway was now attacked at Maan, with serious results to Medina; nevertheless, that city continued to hold out, and was probably never very closely invested.

In October and November, 1917, about the time of the third battle of Gaza, the Turks were still in Maan, and tried to assume the offensive against the Arabs, but proved too weak to succeed. After the fall of Jerusalem, the Turks withdrew to some extent, and the Arabs advanced towards the lands east of the Dead Sea.

From this period forward, the history of the Hejaz revolt merges in that of the Palestine campaign. The Arab forces east of the Dead Sea afforded a safeguard against any possible Turkish attempt to move round our right flank and raid our line of communications. In February and in March, 1918, Turkish expeditions moving against the Arab forces of the King of the Hejaz southward from Kerak, near the south-eastern corner of the Dead Sea, met with failure. The former expedition ended in disaster, and the latter was forced to withdraw, owing to the imminence of a British crossing of the Jordan in its rear. Arab activity on the railway now definitely isolated Medina. Although the Arabs were never strong enough to push a powerful force up through Eastern Palestine, yet the presence of a friendly force operating in that country exercised considerable influence upon the later stages of the Palestine campaign. The assistance which the Arabs gave in the ultimate destruction of the Turkish Army was invaluable.

CHAPTER 4

Palestine

The story of a campaign is more interesting if we have a general idea of the topography of the country in which it is conducted. Our time will, therefore, not be wasted if we leave the British Army on the frontiers of the Holy Land for a few minutes longer and form a mental picture of the terrain over which they are about to operate.

Picture a country, about the size of Wales, divided into parallel strips running north and south, zones of alternate elevation and depression. This will give a rough idea of the conformation of Southern Palestine. On the west is the Mediterranean Sea. Skirting the sea are a series of sand dunes, beyond which comes the Coastal Plain. Together, these form the first depressed strip, averaging about 15 miles in width. Northwards, it tapers to a point where the mountains reach the sea at Cape Carmel. Beyond the Coastal Plain is the range of mountains on which stands Jerusalem, the mountains of Samaria and of Judaea, rising to a height of about 3,000 feet above the level of the sea. On the eastern side of these mountains is a steep drop to the Valley of the Jordan and the Dead Sea, the level of the latter being nearly 1,300 feet below the level of the Mediterranean, and more than 4,000 feet below the summit of the adjoining Mount of Olives. Beyond the Jordan valley the country rises again abruptly into the hills of Moab or Eastern Palestine. Beyond lies the waterless desert.

Before entering into details, let us imagine ourselves to be standing on one of the mountains round about Jerusalem.[1] Away to the north, Mount Carmel rises abruptly from the sea. Thence the chain of Carmel runs S.S.E. for some 20 miles, dividing the Coastal Plain from the Plain of Esdraelon. About Dothan and Tul Keram it merges

1. The point chosen is imaginary. The view described combines those obtainable from two or three points in this neighbourhood.

33

in the range comprising the mountains of Samaria and Judaea, which range runs north and south through the land like the backbone of a fish, with steep spurs, like ribs, thrown out on either side towards the Coastal Plain and the Jordan Valley. Westwards, we look down upon the cultivated plain, and across it to the golden belt of sand dunes, tapering like the waist of an hour-glass where the olive plain touches the sea at Jaffa; beyond, lies the deep blue of the Mediterranean. Eastwards is a sheer abyss falling into the Jordan Valley, where that river, like a silver thread, winds its way along until it falls into the Dead Sea. Beyond, as if across a fifteen-mile moat, rise abruptly the mountains of Moab. The map of Palestine might be aptly compared to a bridge marker. The horizontal line is the plain of Esdraelon. In vertical columns "below the line" lie the strips of the country which we have just described. "Above the line" are the mountains of Lebanon, Tabor and Hermon, Galilee and the Sea of Tiberias, and the valleys and rivers of Damascus.

Let us consider these zones in greater detail, more especially with regard to their influence on war. The sea, which skirts Palestine throughout its length, confers a twofold advantage upon her mistress. In the first place, it provides a supplementary line of communication. We have already seen that, during the advance across the desert, sea-borne supplies from Port Said were landed at El Arish. This method was continued throughout our advance in Palestine, and landing places were improvised at various convenient stages. There is no good harbour along this coast; and landing, which has to be done by beach boats, is difficult, especially in a westerly wind. Nevertheless, considerable supplies were thus landed, chiefly of fuel and fodder, which would be little liable to damage by immersion.

In the second place, help can be given during actual military operations by the navy. Our ships frequently lay off the coast and bombarded the enemy's positions. Of necessity, each side had a flank resting on the sea. To the British, this was a feature of strength; to the Turk, it was one of weakness. He was compelled therefore at all times to draw back or "refuse" his coastal flank, while the British flank was constantly thrown forward menacing the flank of the enemy.

There is little to be said about the sand dunes, though, being on the flank, they were often the scene of operations. The sand here is soft and the going bad. Recourse in these operations was therefore had to camel transport. To the field engineer, difficulties were presented much as in the desert. During the trench warfare before Gaza, when a raid was carried out on Beach Post, no attempt was made to cut the enemy wire with our artillery, but the wire was simply pulled up by hand with the standards, for which the soft sand had provided no firm foundations.

The coastal plain comprises, towards the north, the Biblical Plain of Sharon, and, towards the south, the land of Philistia. By this plain, and not through Judaea, lies the road from the Nile to the Euphrates. Along this plain have marched the invading armies of all the ages. Though generally a flat country, the flatness is relieved by a few rolling hills, of no great height. It is very fertile and has a good supply of water, contained in wells. It thus presents many advantages, and but few disadvantages, to an army operating in the field. Roads are good or are easily improvised, while such obstacles to an invader's advance do not exist here as in the hills. Our successes in the campaign under consideration were generally attained by first pushing forward along the plain and then turning right-handed into the hills.

From the plain, the country rises, in places through the intermediate foot hills of the Shephelah, in places more abruptly and directly into the mountains of Judaea. These mountains are of limestone formation, terraced, where possible, for cultivation, and often wooded with olive trees or tilled as corn patches or vineyards. The scenery is rugged and pretty, the hill-sides generally steep, sometimes precipitous. This is the Palestine of the picture books. Deep gorges have been cut out by water action; but, as no rain falls throughout the summer months, these are, for the most part, but dry watercourses. There are a few good springs to be found in the valleys; the villagers upon the hills are, however, mainly dependent upon cisterns constructed in the rock, in which they catch as much water as possible during the winter rains.

These mountains formed the stronghold of the Israelites, who never maintained sway for any length of time over the lower surrounding country. The mountains abound in ruins and are rich in caves, such as may have been the caves of En-gedi and Adullam. One of the caves witnessed a lurid scene in our mountain fighting. A party of the enemy had established themselves in a cave with machine guns. Ghurkhas attacked, and the enemy, after inflicting casualties, thought to make good their escape by a back exit. But outside there were other Ghurkhas lying in wait, and, as the enemy emerged, they killed them all.

We have seen that the general formation of this range of mountains is like the backbone of a fish. We should therefore expect to find communications from north to south easy enough along the "spine" or ridge, but difficult on either side, where there would be a succession of "ribs" or spurs to be crossed. This is the case. There is only one first-class road from north to south through this hill-country, namely, that which runs along the ridge from Samaria through Nablus, Jerusalem, Bethlehem and Hebron to Beersheba. Communications from east to west are, however, more easy along the spurs and intervening valleys.

To attempt an advance northwards, from spur to spur, is tedious work; after a comparatively short push a pause is necessary to enable roads to be constructed for bringing forward guns and supplies. We had an illustration of this in March, 1918, when a forward move of this character met at first with but moderate opposition. A pause of a few weeks was necessary to enable fresh roads to be made. In the meantime, the enemy had been heavily reinforced, and, when the next advance was attempted, stout resistance was encountered. This hill-country lent itself readily to defence. Mutually supporting heights could be held. A hill, when captured thus, became a focus for fire concentrated from all the hills around. So when the Turks attacked us in these hills they met with much less success than in the Jordan Valley; and, on the other hand, they were able to offer a stouter resistance to our attacks in these hills than they could on the coastal plain.

The Jordan Valley, as we have already seen, is more than a thousand feet below the level of the Mediterranean, that is, below what we speak of as "sea level." In this respect it is unique in the geography of the world. In winter time the climate is equable; in summer it is unbearable. In peace time, even the Bedouin forsake it in summer. The district is pestilential to a degree, and, in no sense of the word, a white man's country. It possesses a feature of considerable importance in the river Jordan itself, almost the only river in Palestine with a perennial flow. The river is tortuous and rapid and not adapted to navigation. These features indicate this area as a difficult one in which to hold a fighting line, and a no less difficult one across which to maintain communications. In the summer of 1918, our line ran along the river valley, and the troops in this sector suffered much from diseases.

East of this strong natural boundary formed by the deep trough of the Jordan, we find a very different country. It rises abruptly from the Jordan Valley, and is in itself a plateau. It is at first fertile, but, at distances ranging from 40 to 60 miles inland, it merges into steppe and then into sheer desert. Thus it is a country apart, difficult of access from Jerusalem and Western Palestine, more easy of access from Damascus or from Arabia. Through it, from north to south, runs the Hejaz railway, on its way from Damascus to Medina. And so it proved an area in which the Turks, based on Damascus, and the Arabs, operating from Hejaz, were at greater advantage than our columns based on Jerusalem.

We have now glanced at those portions of Palestine in which took place the principal fighting in this campaign. Our review would still be incomplete if we omitted all reference to the Plain of Esdraelon. Starting from the sea coast immediately north of Cape Carmel, at the ports of Haifa and Acre, this plain runs east south-east across the country to the Jordan Valley. Rising slightly at first, it forms the watershed of "that ancient river, the river Kishon." After the watershed is crossed, there is a drop towards the Jordan Valley; this latter portion of the plain constitutes the Vale of Jezreel. This Plain of Esdraelon is Armageddon. Here Barak overthrew Sisera, Gideon defeated the Midianites, and Saul and Jonathan met disaster and death at the hands of the Philistines. Here Josiah was defeated and slain by Pharaoh Necho. Near here, the Christians were defeated and their kingdom overthrown by the Saracens. On this plain Napoleon won his final and crushing victory over the Turks.

No battle, beyond a few cavalry engagements, took place here during the campaign which we are to consider. The Turks had been totally defeated before ever this line was reached. But this plain has still for us a military interest. It may well be that here, where the mountains of Samaria overlook and command all approaches from the north, is to be found the best strategic line for the defence of the Suez Canal.

In a country like Palestine, where levels and characteristics are so divergent, diversities of climate are to be expected. We have seen that the summer climate of the Lower Jordan Valley is pestilential. Parts of the coastal plain also are very malarious, particularly from north of Jaffa to Mount Carmel. With these exceptions, the climate is by no means unpleasant nor unsuitable for the conduct of military operations. Far enough south to enjoy plenty of bright sunshine, it is still some distance north of the tropics. Pleasant and regular breezes from the sea mitigate the discomfort which might otherwise prevail in a country almost surrounded by desert.

The whole of the rainfall comes in the winter months. From about April to October, though dews are heavy, rain is unknown. But in the winter months, especially December and January, and to some extent

February, the rainfall is intense, and the country on the plains and lower lying districts is reduced to a sea of mud well-nigh impassable. Thus military operations in summer are liable to be prejudiced by a shortage of water; in winter by an excess. The ideal season for operations is therefore in the spring, when there is an abundance of water and a plentiful feed; and, next to this, the autumn, when the heat of the summer has passed its height and the rains of winter have not yet made the country impassable.

The importance of good railways in modern war is immense. We have already traced the construction of the broad gauge line from Egypt which followed close behind the British in their advance across the desert and into Southern Palestine. The Turks in Western Palestine were at a perpetual disadvantage through the inferiority of the railway service; but, in Eastern Palestine, i.e. across the Jordan, the position was reversed. Before the war, Syria had been connected with Asia Minor by a broad gauge line from Aleppo to Rayak, where it effected a junction with a narrow gauge line from Beyrout to Damascus. The broad gauge line was part of the Baghdad railway scheme. But at this time, that railway, even between Constantinople and Aleppo, was only partially completed.

The tunnelling of the Taurus Mountains was yet unfinished. Thus troops or supplies, coming from Constantinople to Damascus, had to break the journey at the Taurus Mountains and again at Rayak. These two interruptions provided admirable opportunities for delay and confusion, which the dilatory Turk embraced. The tunnelling of the Taurus was pushed on with during the war, and in 1918 rumours reached us that these mountains had been pierced, so that trains could then run through from Constantinople (Haida Pasha) to Rayak. The installation of more business-like Germans at the latter station went far towards minimising the delays and confusion due to the break of gauge.

From Damascus, the Hejaz railway, constructed nominally for Mecca pilgrims, runs due south, and, passing along the high plateau of Eastern Palestine, had already reached Medina. A branch from this line, starting from a junction at Deraa, ran westwards along the Plain of Esdraelon to Haifa. Another line, almost parallel to the Hejaz railway, ran from Damascus due south to Mezerib; this line was removed by the Turks after the commencement of the war, as the materials were required for railway construction elsewhere. Unconnected with any of these railways, a French line ran from Jaffa to Jerusalem; this also the Turks removed, as between Jaffa and Ludd, while, for the remainder of its length, they altered the gauge so as to adapt it to the rolling stock of the Hejaz Railway. All these railways south of Damascus were narrow-gauge lines, without much rolling stock available, so that their carrying capacity was limited.

On the outbreak of war, the Turks, acting under the guidance of the Germans, embarked upon a considerable programme of railway construction. Starting from a point on the Plain of Esdraelon, El Apele, they constructed a new line which crossed the mountains about Samaria and reached the Plain of Sharon at Tul Keram. Thence it ran down the length of the coastal plain to Beersheba, and, ultimately, to Auja in the desert. This railway was constructed in 1915 for the invasion of Egypt. Into this railway was incorporated portions of the old Jaffa-Jerusalem line, as between Ludd and "Junction Station." This was the none too distinctive name given to the important station which was constructed at the point where the older railway left the plain; this now became the junction for Jerusalem. At a later date, the Turks withdrew from Auja to Beersheba, the line south of the latter place was removed and a new line was constructed from near Junction Station to points just north of Gaza.

Roads in the coastal sector are good, though difficult for heavy motor traffic after rain. In the hills, the only first-class roads were the road running north and south along the ridge from Nablus through Jerusalem to Beersheba, and the road west and east from Jaffa to Jerusalem, continued eastwards through Jericho and across the Jordan to Es Salt and Amman Station on the Hejaz Railway.

The population of Palestine is very mixed, comprising Moslems, Christians and Jews with their various subdivisions and sects. The Moslem inhabitants, Arabs and Syrians, have little in common with the Turks except their religion. The Jews and the Christians groaned under Turkish oppression. Both Jews and Christians welcomed the advent of the British, while the Moslems accepted the situation, if not with pleasure, at least with equanimity. The Turks themselves form no part of the regular population. They are alien rulers, speaking a language unknown to the people, and incapable of understanding the language of the country. Although Palestine has been governed by Moslems for upwards of a thousand years, it has only been annexed to the Ottoman Empire for four centuries. More than once during that period it would have been torn away but for the aid of the British. The government of Syria by the Ottoman Turk had been oppressive and corrupt and marked by the discouragement of all progress and enterprise. It was high time that it should cease.

CHAPTER 5

Gaza

Gaza! What pictures this name conjures up in our imagination. From childhood the city has been familiar to us for its dramatic associations with Samson. It was here that he removed the city gates and carried them to the summit of Ali Muntar, "to the top of an hill that is before Hebron," and it was here that he took hold of the two middle pillars, and, bowing himself with all his might, destroyed the temple of Dagon with the thousands of Philistines that were his tormentors. The whole history of Gaza is steeped in blood. It is the outpost of Africa, the gate of Asia. Throughout the ages its strategic importance has been immense. Scarcely an invading army has passed here without fighting a battle. It figured in the wars of the Eastern invaders, was totally destroyed by Alexander the Great, was the scene of one of Napoleon's battles, and, during our campaign, saw six months of trench warfare and no less than three distinct and sanguinary engagements. In the course of its history, Gaza is said to have been taken and destroyed in war between forty and fifty times. No city in the world has been destroyed more often. Happy, indeed is the city that has no history!

Prior to this war, Gaza was a town of some 40,000 inhabitants, mostly Moslems, to whom the city is sacred. It owed its importance in modern times to being the junction of the caravan routes from Egypt to Syria and from Arabia to the Mediterranean. The town itself stands back some couple of miles from the sea, from which it is separated by sand dunes. It is surrounded by gardens and plantations; most of these are bordered by thick cactus hedges, which played a prominent part in the days of trench warfare. The surrounding country is by no means level, but consists of rolling arable land with low ridges and some hills. The most prominent feature is the hill, Ali Muntar, a commanding height south-east of the town. When we first approached it, the hill was clad with trees and surrounded by a tomb; but six months' persistent bombardment soon removed the trees and tomb and altered the conformation of the hill. There are other ridges lying about the town, which were afterwards incorporated in the defensive schemes of the Turks and of ourselves.

The geographical feature of principal military importance in this neighbourhood is the Wadi Ghuzzeh. This *wadi* is a watercourse, which, in times of rain, carries off the water from the hills between Beersheba and the Dead Sea. It runs, approximately, from south-east to north-west, at right angles to the coast line, and passes Gaza at a distance of about 4 miles from the south-western or Egyptian side of the town. During the greater part of the year this watercourse is dry, though the sides are steep, and wheeled traffic can only cross at properly constructed crossings. On either side of this *wadi*, distant a mile or so from its bed, are ridges which run approximately parallel to the *wadi*. That on the right bank is known as Mansura Ridge, that on the left bank as In Seirat. The latter is a relatively high ridge and affords cover for troops beyond. On the other side of this ridge, protected by it, and distant some nine or ten miles from Gaza, is a small village with a good supply of water. This village is known as Deir el Belah, or, more frequently, merely as Belah. It formed our advanced base during the later operations against Gaza.

We have seen that, at the end of February, 1917, General Dobell's force had reached El Arish, while portions of it had crossed the border at Rafa, and his cavalry had occupied Khan Yunus. The Turks had withdrawn to Gaza, where they now took up a position. They had one force at Gaza and another in the neighbourhood of Beersheba, with other troops between. In March, it was decided to attack the enemy at Gaza. The British force was concentrated at Rafa, whence it marched up secretly by night. On the night of the 25th March, it moved forward from Belah against the first objective, the In Seirat Ridge. This was secured without serious opposition. There was a dense fog on the morning of the 26th, and, as the troops were moving through standing crops, finding the way was none too easy. However, the Wadi Ghuzzeh was crossed, and the high ground at Mansura Ridge was secured.

From there, an attack was delivered across the open against Ali Muntar and Gaza. The main attack was made by the 53rd Division, plus one brigade of the 54th, while the 52nd Division were in reserve. Our troops captured, and established themselves on Ali Muntar, and also on the hill beyond, known as Australia Hill. From these points they looked down upon and dominated the town of Gaza. Meanwhile, the cavalry had been ordered to go round by the right, and to cut off the enemy when he should retreat. The cavalry not only got round, but succeeded in entering the town itself, where they captured some of the Turkish staff. The Turks believed that the game was up, and were now preparing to surrender.

It was the opinion of many who took part in the battle, that, had we held on for a short time longer, we should have captured the town and the whole of this force, and that we should have then been in a position to meet and to defeat the enemy reinforcements, since the 52nd Division in reserve had not yet been brought into action. However, Turkish reinforcements were now reported to be coming up from the direction of Beersheba, and to be threatening our right flank. Accordingly, a withdrawal was ordered, and our troops fell back on the Mansura Ridge, the New Zealanders coming right through the town of Gaza itself. That night, orders were given for an immediate retirement, and our forces recrossed the Wadi Ghuzzeh. The bulk of the force retired to Belah, while outposts held the In Seirat Ridge. After a two days' battle, wherein complete success had been almost within our grasp, we had but little to show save casualties.

From the summit of In Seirat Ridge, a commanding view is obtained over the whole country from Gaza to Beersheba. From this point of vantage the Turks could be seen, throughout the first fortnight in April, busily digging themselves in and wiring their positions. We, on our side, were no less assiduous in preparations for another battle. Patrols were sent out to reconnoitre the country, and working parties went out into No Man's Land to construct ramparts and make all preparations for getting guns across the Wadi Ghuzzeh. The 74th Division were brought up to Belah. A few of the newly invented "tanks" arrived from England, and aroused great expectations.

The day of the second battle of Gaza arrived. On the 16th April, the force moved out from Belah and crossed the Wadi Ghuzzeh by night. On this occasion, the first objective was Mansura Ridge, which was captured without much difficulty. The second, and principal objective, was the strong line of Turkish positions to the south and southeast of Gaza, and fronting the Gaza-Beersheba road. The troops detailed for the attack were the 52nd, the 53rd and the 54th Divisions, the 54th to move forward from Mansura, the 52nd on their left and the 53rd close to the sea. It was contemplated that most of our difficulties would be obviated by a long artillery preparation and by the newly arrived tanks which had acquired a high reputation in France. Accordingly, the enemy positions were shelled for two hours, and then the infantry advanced, preceded by these tanks. But, alas, the tanks were few in number; some were soon put out of action, or caught fire; and the hopes that they had raised were disappointed.

The infantry advanced over some 3,000 yards of perfectly open plain, until they reached the enemy's uncut wire; here they were mown down by the enemy's machine guns. That night, those that were able to do so, crept back under cover of darkness to Mansura Ridge. The dead lay where they fell, a gruesome spectacle, for over six months, until buried by our own parties after the third battle of Gaza. Those that returned were collected and reorganized at Mansura Ridge, and at once commenced to dig in at this position. This was the night of the 19th April.

Next morning, the Turks came pouring out of their positions to gloat over their success. By this time we had done little more than scratch the surface; had the Turks closed to deliver a determined counter-attack, they might have made matters distinctly uncomfortable. As it was, they came out merely as spectators. Our guns opened upon them and they withdrew. After this, our digging proceeded apace, and we soon had a satisfactory position entrenched from Mansura to the sea.

There is a saying in the East that the British always come back, meaning that reverses only make them more determined to try again and to succeed. Thus did the British come back into the Soudan, and into the Transvaal. Thus was the surrender of Kut wiped out by the capture of Baghdad. And so were our losses at Gaza in this spring avenged by our victory on these same battlefields in the following autumn. For the time being, however, both sides settled down to the routine life of modern trench warfare.

Now followed a complete reorganization of our army in Egypt. On the 28th June, 1917, the post of Commander-in-Chief of the Egyptian Expeditionary Force was taken over by General Sir Edmund Allenby, G.C.M.G., K.C.B. The organization into an Eastern Force under a subordinate commander, which had been instituted in the summer of 1916, was abolished, and the force was organized in Corps. The strength of the Egyptian Expeditionary Force was augmented, much artillery being added, besides three divisions of infantry. The 10th (Irish) and the 60th (London) Divisions were brought across from Salonica. The 75th Division was organized in the country and consisted of four battalions of Indian troops, taken from the Suez Canal Zone defences, and nine battalions of West of England Territorials, that had been in the East since the beginning of the war, and had, for the most part, been garrisoning India.

When this reorganization was complete, this army was constituted as follows: The 20th Corps, comprising the 10th (Irish), the 53rd (Welsh), the 60th (London) and the 74th (Dismounted Yeomanry) Divisions. The 21st Corps, comprising the 52nd (Scottish Lowland), the 54th (East Anglian) and the 75th (Wessex and Indian) Divisions. The Desert Mounted Corps, comprising the Australian Mounted Division, the Anzac Mounted Division and the Yeomanry Division. General Allenby had, as his chief-of-staff, Major-General L. J. Bols, C.B., D.S.O. In addition to the above troops, there was, on this front, a composite brigade, consisting of French and Italians, familiarly known as the "Mixed Vermouth" Brigade. Other regiments were represented, such as Indian Imperial troops, and battalions of the British West India Regiment, while representative units of the Egyptian Army did duty upon the Lines of Communication.

Although each division was associated with some particular portion of Great Britain, from which it took its name, the association was not exclusive. Thus, the 52nd Lowland Division had at least one Highland Battalion, the 53rd Welsh had more battalions from England than from Wales, and the 54th East Anglian contained one battalion from London and one from the South of England. It will be best, therefore, if, in our future pages, we refer to divisions only by number.

An interesting feature about General Allenby's army was that, from this time forward, the greater portion consisted of Territorials.

CHAPTER 6

Trench Warfare

It was in the late summer of 1917 that the regiment with which I was serving joined the Expeditionary Force. Coming from India, we landed at Suez and were railed through at once to Kantara. This place we found a hive of industry, as befitted the military base of so important an expedition. Like other units similarly arriving from India, we were kept here for a fortnight. This time was devoted to the equipping of the battalion on the scale applicable to this country, with transport, draught and riding animals, Lewis guns and such other equipment as we required for the operations on which we were to embark.

Immediately we were ready to move, we were railed up to the Front, to Belah, which, at that time, was railhead. This was our first experience of travelling on the Kantara Military Railway, and is not likely to be forgotten. The shortage of rolling stock available did not permit of troops, or, at that time, even of officers accompanying troops, travelling in passenger coaches. On the contrary, a number of open trucks were adapted for troop traffic, being roofed over with a covering affording protection from the sun but with sides left open. These trucks had neither continuous brakes nor screw couplings.

Our journey, therefore, was enlivened by the frequent successful attempts of our truck to overtake the truck ahead, followed by a difference of opinion with the truck behind, a wavering between two opinions, and then another mad plunge into the darkness in pursuit of the truck ahead, and the next check brought about a repetition of this pleasing diversion from sleep. If the writer of a recent popular song really believed that the Sands of the Desert never grow cold, let him try travelling across them by night in an open truck. The train was not furnished with that luxury of modern travel, steam heating. For the men, a substitute was found by adopting the method by which sheep

45

are kept cosy on similar occasions, that is, by packing into each truck a few more than it can accommodate. The officers rolled themselves up in their valises, bruised every protruding bone in their bodies, "and wished for the day."

On arrival at the front, we moved first into a position in reserve near the Wadi Ghuzzeh. As we crossed the summit of In Seirat Ridge, what a view unfolded itself before our eyes! Before us lay the Plain of Philistia, spreading from the sea to the Judaean Hills, to our left front lay the white buildings of the town of Gaza, while, ever and anon, were heard and seen the booming of cannon and the bursting of shell.

We were now put through a gradual process of acclimatization. Ensconced in one of the offshoots of the Wadi Ghuzzeh well behind the front line, we enjoyed safety from shelling. We were, however, sufficiently in the picture to have guns constantly firing around us and aeroplanes flying overhead, and could watch our friends being shelled in the front line and the daily anti-aeroplane shoots, both by our own and by the enemy's "Archies." Here we were able to carry out a certain amount of training, and to organize the battalion upon the lines of the new "normal formation," giving the platoon commander control over each kind of weapon with which the infantry are armed—rifle, bayonet, bomb, rifle-bomb and Lewis gun. Gas masks were issued, and all ranks were instructed in their use.

In a couple of weeks this training, or rather adaptation of our previous training to the conditions of trench warfare upon this front, had so far progressed that we could enter upon the next stage of our acclimatization. Individual companies were now sent up into the front line "for instruction." This consisted of their being attached to other units that were garrisoning the front line. Our men were posted in the trenches with men of such other units; and some of the officers and men accompanied patrols into "No Man's Land." After three weeks of acclimatization, we moved up to the front line and ourselves took over a section of the defences. And here we remained until after the fall of Gaza.

The Turkish Army at this time, as we have seen, held a strong position from the sea at Gaza, roughly along the main Gaza-Beersheba road to Beersheba. His force was on a wide front, the distance from Gaza to Beersheba being about 30 miles. Gaza itself had been made into a strong modern fortress, heavily entrenched and wired, offering every facility for protracted defence. The civilian population had been evacuated. The remainder of the enemy's line consisted originally of a series of strong localities, which were known as the Sihan group of works, the Atawinah group, the Baha group, the Abu Hareira-Arab el Teeaha trench system, and finally, the works covering Beersheba. During the period from July to October, the defences had been considerably strengthened, and these strong localities had, by the end of October, been joined up to form a practically continuous line from the sea to a point south of Sheria, except for a gap of some 1,500 to 2,000 yards between Ali Muntar and the Sihan group.

The defensive works round Beersheba remained a detached system, but had been improved and extended. A new railway had been made from El Tine, just south of Junction Station on the Damascus-Beersheba railway to Beit Hanun, just north of Gaza, with a subsidiary branch to Huj, the latter intended to supply the centre of the defensive line. It was evident, therefore, that the enemy was determined to make every effort to maintain his position on the Gaza-Beersheba line.

The British force was extended on a front of 22 miles from the sea opposite Gaza to Gamli. About 6 miles inland, the Wadi Ghuzzeh is joined by a short tributary *wadi*, on the right bank, known as the Wadi Nukhabir. The point at which this *wadi* commenced was about a mile or so nearer to the enemy than the line of our positions opposite Gaza. Its headaters (to use an expression scarcely appropriate to a dry watercourse) were within the apex of a **V**-shaped escarpment, the point of the **V** protruding towards the enemy. The feature might be compared to a heel-mark in soft ground. On the convex side were slight ridges with gentle forward slopes; on the concave were steep escarpments. The ridges of the **V** were known as Mansura and Sheikh Abbas Ridges respectively; the point was merely known as "The Apex."

Our trench system here ran along the forward slopes of these ridges, a hundred yards or so below the crest, whence the country fell towards the enemy in a gentle glacis slope devoid of cover. Our reserves and our day positions were behind the escarpment, where was excellent cover from hostile shelling. The portion of the enemy's works in front of this sector was the Sihan group, a strongly prepared position distant about a mile. The apex itself formed a salient, necessary to hold since its Ridges would otherwise have dominated our positions; but, though a salient, the position was undoubtedly strong. The situation and the conformation of the Apex, therefore, both invited attack and assisted defence. From the sea to the Apex we had a continuous line of trenches. Beyond Sheikh Abbas our defences consisted of a series of redoubts, our right flank being to some extent in the air. Here, however, was a waterless desert, so difficult to cross that this flank could be sufficiently protected by cavalry patrols.

Considering that there was a war on, campaigning life on this front was by no means uncomfortable. Those who had seen service in France bemoaned the lack of comforts and amusements behind the line, and the absence of home leave, those who had come from Salonica were congratulating themselves on the exchange; while those of us who had been in Mesopotamia during the bad times of 1916, considered ourselves in the lap of luxury. Rations were good and plentiful and canteen well stocked. The Turkish rations, on the other hand, were scanty and poor, with the result that morale was low, discomfort rife, and desertions frequent.

On one occasion, when the enemy were making a raid upon our trenches, a couple of Turks got into an empty bag where one of our men had left his pack. The manner in which they pursued their advantage was by helping themselves to his tin of bully beef and getting away with all speed. A Turkish officer, who was subsequently taken prisoner, said, "If the Turkish rations had been as good as yours, you would never have captured Gaza."

The health of our troops, on the whole, was good. In so far as there was sickness it consisted of a certain amount of dysentery, almost unavoidable in an army in the field, septic sores, which are unusually rife, and a slight epidemic of sandfly fever. Foremost among the inconveniences to be tolerated were the flies, which made it difficult for the men to sleep by day, the time when they most need rest after manning the trenches all night. Next to the flies came the dust. The country, in which for the time we were making our home, consisted of arable ground devoid of crops, and thoroughly cut up by the passing of transport. A breeze, that blew daily without fail, served to raise a fine impalpable dust that permeated everything. This powder dust made marching difficult, but wise forethought caused galvanized iron netting to be laid along all the principal routes, forming "wire roads" for the use of light motor-cars and "foot-sloggers." If we grumbled at the dust, we had, at this time at least, no cause to complain, like our brethren in Flanders, of the mud. Taken all together, the morale was good and the men distinctly happy.

Life in these days was not without its diversions and touches of humour. A nice Roman tessellated pavement was unearthed near the Wadi Ghuzzeh, at the place called Umm Jerar, which is associated with Abraham. Going one day to look for it, I found a military police-man on duty within half a mile of the spot. I said to him, "Can you tell me the way to the tessellated pavement?"

He looked at me vacantly for a minute and then replied: "Is it the wire road that you happen to mean, sir?"

On one occasion, the general was going round the front line ac-companied by the intelligence officer (who is the officer that selects the pass-word which is changed daily) and by the C.O. of the unit in this sector. Staying out rather later than they had intended, it was dusk or dark when they approached one of the posts.

The sentry challenged, "Halt—hands up." Up went the general's hands in prompt compliance.

"Advance one, and give the countersign," continued the sentry.

The general turned to the intelligence officer, "What is the coun-tersign today?" said he.

"Really I am afraid I have forgotten," replied the intelligence of-ficer, and both referred to the colonel.

"When I left my headquarters, it had not yet come through," was his reply.

The sentry remained obdurate. Then followed explanations, and, after some parley and identifications, the party were allowed to pro-ceed.

As they were leaving, the general hurried again to the sentry, say-ing, "Well, my man, you might just tell us now what the password is."

"I am sorry, sir," was his reply, "but I haven't the least idea."

About this time the spy peril was rather rife. We had orders not to leave our lines without revolvers, for protection against assassination by spies. To one particular "hush-hush" spot rode up a general with his staff officer, both faultlessly attired, accompanied by the usual orderly. The general asked to be shown round, and his request was conceded with the thoroughness and courtesy due to his high rank. His inspec-tion completed, the general expressed his thanks, and the party rode away, never to be heard of again,—at least not in that capacity. Shortly afterwards, a notorious spy was seen working as a *coolie* in the Egyptian Labour Corps. Perhaps he was the general.

The monotony of trench life was varied by occasional raids into the enemy trenches. Some very successful raids were carried out on the enemy's defences near the sea, especially at Beach Post, and other successful raids were made from the Apex upon the advanced trenches of the Sihan group of works. Mutual bombardments frequently enlivened the proceedings, the supremacy in which undoubtedly lay with our artillery. These never allowed a day to pass without doing some firing, and they had sniping guns ever ready to fire on any movement that might be seen in enemy territory. The enemy guns, largely manned by Austrians, reserved their fire for concentrated bombardments; evidently they were less able to replenish their supplies of ammunition.

The sector of the front line which fell to our lot to hold was a portion of the Apex. Our front line companies manned a continuous system of trenches, while the reserve company and headquarters occupied dugouts dug into, or constructed with sand bags upon, the steep slopes of the escarpment. There were deep tunnel dugouts, extending into the bowels of the earth, in the support area, but these were never used. In the front line there were no such dug-outs, except for such purposes as signal office and platoon headquarters. In case of intense shelling, the front line garrison, except sentries, could obtain fair cover behind the traverses in the narrow trenches which connected up the wider and more exposed fire bays.

It is a debatable question whether deep dugouts in or near the front line are advisable. When the enemy shells intensively, if he means business, his barrage is closely followed by his infantry. When the barrage lifts, therefore, it is of vital importance to man the fire-step immediately. It is not easy to turn a large number of men quickly out of deep dugouts which may thus prove only a fool's paradise. In one of the raids made near the sea, our infantry, following closely up to the barrage, caught the enemy taking refuge in dugouts, and had no difficulty in capturing or accounting for the whole garrison of the raided trench. At the Apex we were three times bombarded and raided. On each occasion the garrison merely took refuge behind the traverses. Although they endured it, the bombardment was much more uncomfortable here than if the men had been in good dugouts; yet they were able to man the trenches so quickly that in no case could the enemy effect a lodgement, and in only one case did he even reach the trench.

When we took over the Apex, the days of sporadic raids by us were past, and all thought was concentrated on preparations for the great day that was then imminent. On the other hand, there was great patrolling activity. Our officers' patrols went out nightly into No Man's Land, and brought back information as to enemy works in progress and activity in their trenches. These patrols had many exciting experiences, and, in the dark, frequently encountered patrols sent out by the enemy. Much useful information was brought in by these patrols to the battalions holding this sector of the line, especially during the first few days after the commencement of the great offensive which resulted in the capture of Gaza and Beersheba.

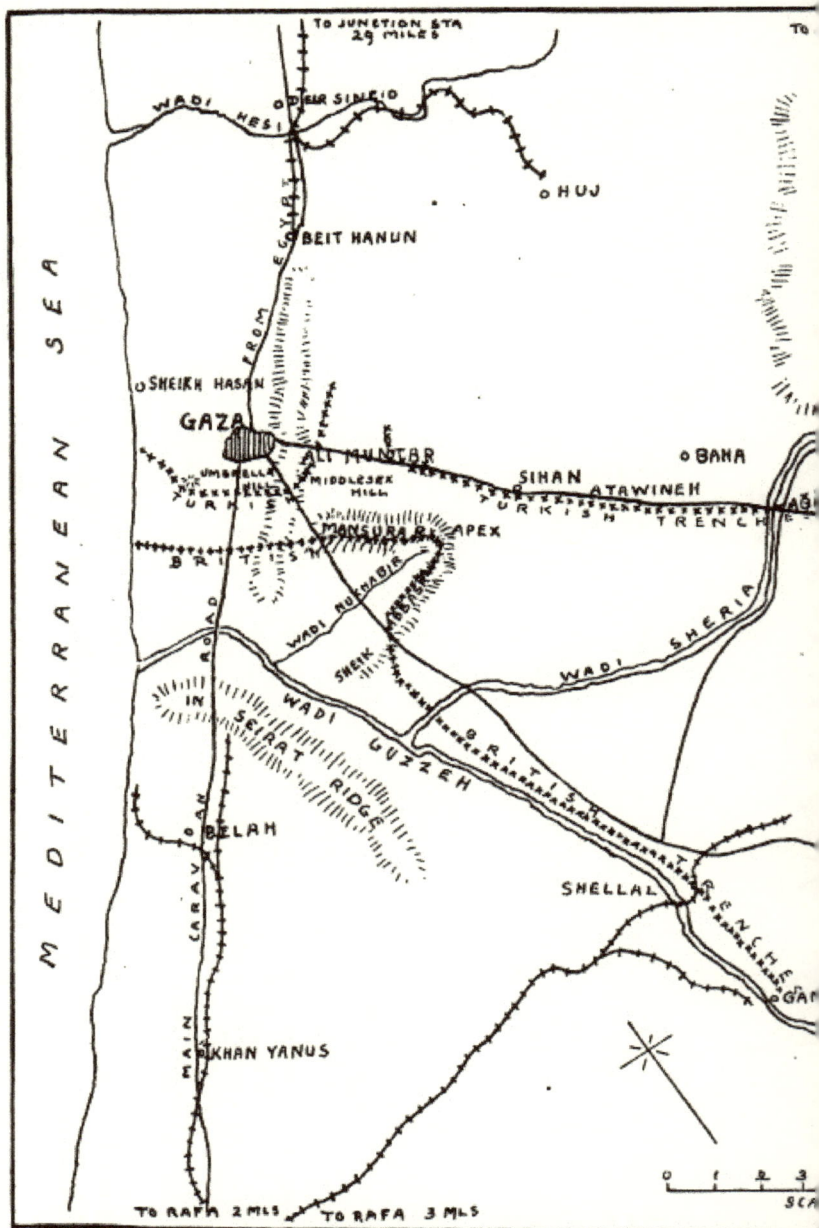

SKETCH MAP

OF COUNTRY ROUND GAZA
AND BEERSHEBA

ILLUSTRATING OPERATIONS FROM
MARCH TO NOVEMBER 1917

TO HEBRON
15 MILES

ON STA.
MILES

RIA

TOM AL
ABU JERWAL

oMUWEILEH

ARAB EL TEIAHA

KK

HAUWUKAH

EIRA

EL SEBA

IRGEIG

BEERSHEBA

GIRHEIR

TO AUJA
40. MLS

(1070)
S H

KARM

BUGGAR

ESANA

oKHALASA

5   10 MILES

1/250,000

TO AUJA
20 MILES

CHAPTER 7

Gaza and Beersheba

The plan by which General Allenby defeated the Turks and captured their Gaza–Beersheba line, involved three distinct operations. It will be remembered that the enemy defences consisted of a substantially continuous line from the sea at Gaza to Arab el Teeaha, where the left flank was bent back or "refused" at or about Sheria. Some 4½ miles farther on were the detached works covering Beersheba, which thus constituted a strong outwork protecting the left flank of the main position. The decisive blow was to be struck against the left flank of the main Turkish position at Hareira and Sheria. Before this blow could be struck, it was necessary to clear away the obstacle presented by Beersheba. It was also necessary to keep the enemy in doubt as to where the decisive blow was to fall; so another operation, on as large a scale as the available force would permit, and calculated both to mystify the enemy and to draw off a portion of his reserves, was undertaken on the immediate sea front at Gaza. Thus we get, firstly, the capture of Beersheba; secondly, the attack on the Gaza coastal defences; and, thirdly, the main attack delivered against Sheria.

This plan of operations was chosen for the following reasons. The enemy's works in the Hareira-Sheria sector were less formidable than elsewhere, and they were easier of approach than other parts of the enemy's defences. The capture of Beersheba was a necessary preliminary to the main operation, in order to secure the water supply at that place, and to give room for the deployment of the attacking force on the high ground to the north and north-west of Beersheba, from which direction the main attack was to be developed. When Beersheba was in our hands, we should have an open flank against which to operate, and full use could be made of our superiority in mounted troops. Moreover, a success here offered prospects of pursuing our advantage, and forcing the enemy to abandon the rest of his fortified positions, which no other line of attack would afford.

The difficulties to be overcome in the operations against Beersheba and the Hareira-Sheria line were considerable. Foremost among them were our old friend, the shortage of water, and, scarcely less formidable, the difficulty of transport.

With regard to water, no supply existed in the area over which operations were to take place.

An ample supply of water was known to exist at Beersheba, but it was uncertain how quickly it could be developed or to what extent the enemy would have damaged the wells before we succeeded in occupying the town. Except at Beersheba, no large supply of water would be found till Sheria and Hareira had been captured. Arrangements had therefore to be made to ensure that the troops could be kept supplied with water, while operating at considerable distances from their original water base, for a period which might amount to a week or more.

This was to some extent met by developing the water supplies at Ecani, Khalassa and Asluj, all places in No Man's Land some miles beyond our right flank.

The transport problem was no less difficult. Beersheba, itself some thousand feet above the sea level, lies in a recess on the western slopes of the Judaean Hills. In the bed of this recess runs the Wadi Es Saba. Towards the north-east a good metalled road leads gradually to the summit of the hills and on through Hebron to Jerusalem. Northwest a good road led along the enemy's front to Gaza. The railway line, avoiding the heights, for the first ten or twelve miles follows approximately the direction of the Gaza road, and then turns northwards along the Plain or Foothills. But south of the Gaza-Beersheba line there were no good roads, "and no reliance could therefore be placed on the use of motor transport." Owing to the steep banks of many of the *wadis* which intersected the area of operations, the routes passable by wheeled transport were limited, and, in many places, the going was heavy and difficult.

Practically the whole of the transport available in the force, including 30,000 pack camels, had to be allotted to one portion of the eastern force, to enable it to be kept supplied with food, water and ammunition, at a distance of 15 to 20 miles in advance of railhead.

There already existed a branch from the Kantara military railway; which branch, leaving the main line at Rafa, ran to Shellal and Gamli, supplying the right of our line. Arrangements were made for this railhead to be pushed forward as rapidly as possible from Shellal towards Karm (some 7 miles to the east-south-east of Shellal), and for a line to be laid from Gamli towards Beersheba for the transport of ammunition. No Man's Land being some 10 or 12 miles wide in this sector, railway construction was carried on in front of our front line under cover of yeomanry outposts.

This line of outposts was attacked on the morning of the 27th October by a strong reconnoitring party that the Turks sent out from the direction of Kauwukah to make a reconnaissance towards Karm. On a division of our infantry coming up, the Turks withdrew.

By the end of October all our preparations were ready. The bombardment of the Gaza defences commenced on the 27th and continued nightly. On the 30th, warships of the Royal Navy, assisted by a French battleship, began co-operating in this bombardment. The actual infantry attack on Gaza was not intended to take place, however, until after the capture of Beersheba, and was delayed accordingly.

The date fixed for the attack on Beersheba was the 31st October. The plan was to attack with two divisions the hostile works between the Khalassa Road and the Wadi Saba, that is, the sector to the southwest of the town. The works north of the Wadi Saba were to be masked with the Imperial Camel Corps and some infantry, while a portion of the 53rd Division further north covered the left of the Corps. The right of the attack was covered by a cavalry regiment. Further east, mounted troops took up a line opposite the southern defences of Beersheba. A mounted force, starting from Khalassa and Asluj, beyond our original right flank, were detailed to make a wide flanking movement and attack Beersheba from the east and north-east.

The units detailed for the attack moved by a night march, and were in their appointed positions by dawn of the 31st. As a preliminary to the main attack, in order to enable field guns to be brought within effective range for wire-cutting, an attack was made upon the enemy's advanced works on the high ground about a couple of miles south-west of the town, at Hill 1070. This had been successfully accomplished by 8.45 a.m., and the cutting of the wire proceeded satisfactorily, though pauses had to be made to allow the dust to clear. The assault was ordered for 12.15 p.m., and proved successful. By about

10 p.m., the whole of the works between the Khalassa Road and the Wadi Saba were in our hands.

Meanwhile the mounted troops, after a night march of, for a portion of the force, some 35 miles, arrived early on this same morning, the 31st, at about Khasim Zanna, in the hills, some 5 miles east of Beersheba. From the hills, the advance into Beersheba from the east and north-east lies over an open and almost flat plain, commanded by the rising ground north of the town and flanked by an underfeature in the Wadi Saba, called Tel el Saba.

A force was sent north to secure Bir es Sakaly, on the Hebron Road, and protect the right flank. This force met with some opposition, and was engaged with hostile cavalry at Bir es Sakaly and to the north during the day. Tel el Saba was found strongly held by the enemy, and was not captured till late in the afternoon.

Meanwhile, attempts to advance in small parties across the plain towards the town made slow progress. In the evening, however, a mounted attack by Australian Light Horse, who rode straight at the town from the East, proved completely successful. They galloped over two deep trenches held by the enemy just outside the town, and entered the town at about 7 p.m., capturing numerous prisoners.

A very strong position was thus taken with slight loss, and the Turkish detachment at Beersheba almost completely put out of action. This success laid open the left flank of the main Turkish position for a decisive blow.

The actual date of the attack at Gaza had been left open till the result of the attack at Beersheba was known, as it was intended that the attack on Gaza, which was designed to draw hostile reserves towards that sector, should take place a day or two before the attack on the Sheria position. After the complete success of the Beersheba operations, it was decided that the attack on Gaza should take place on the morning of the 2nd November.

The objectives of this attack were the hostile works from Umbrella Hill (2,000 yards south-west of the town) to Sheikh Hasan, on the sea (about 2,500 yards north-west of the town). The front of the attack was about 6,000 yards, and Sheikh Hasan, the farthest objective, was over 3,000 yards from our front line.

The ground over which the attack took place consisted of sand dunes, rising in places up to 150 feet in height. This sand is very deep and heavy going. The enemy's defences consisted of several lines of strongly built trenches and redoubts.

As Umbrella Hill flanked the advance against the Turkish works farther west, it was decided to capture it by a preliminary operation, to take place four hours previous to the main attack. It was accordingly attacked and captured at 11.0 p.m. on the 1st November by a portion of the 52nd Division. This attack drew a heavy bombardment of Umbrella Hill itself and our front lines, which lasted for two hours, but ceased in time to allow the main attack, which was timed for 3.0 a.m., to form up without interference.

This attack partook of the nature of a modern trench to trench advance, as seen on the battlefields of France, with the co-operation of tanks and the accompaniment of other products of modern science. It was successful in reaching most of its objectives. The enemy losses were heavy, especially from the preliminary bombardment.

Subsequent reports from prisoners stated that one of the divisions holding the Gaza Sector was withdrawn on account of casualties, a Division from the general reserve being drawn into this Sector to replace it. The attack thus succeeded in its primary object, which was to prevent any units being withdrawn from the Gaza defences to meet the threat to the Turkish left flank and to draw into Gaza as large a proportion as possible of the available Turkish reserves. Further, the capture of Sheikh Hasan and the south-western defences constituted a very direct threat to the whole of the Gaza position, which could be developed on any sign of a withdrawal on the part of the enemy.

Here the force attacking Gaza stayed its hand, merely holding on to the positions already captured, while the main attack was being developed on the right.

Having captured Beersheba on the 31st October, a force was pushed out early on the following day, the 1st November, into the hills north of Beersheba, with the object of securing the flank of the attack on Sheria, while mounted troops were sent north along the Hebron road. Accordingly, the 53rd Division took up a position from Towal Abu Jerwal (6 miles north of Beersheba) to Muweileh (3½ miles farther west and the 10th Division occupied Abu Irgeig, on the railway, 6 miles from Beersheba.

Next day, the 2nd, our mounted troops found and engaged considerable enemy forces to the north of Towal Abu Jerwal. Accordingly, on the 3rd, we advanced in that direction towards Ain Kohleh and Khuweilfeh, where the enemy were found to be holding a strong position with considerable and increasing forces. It will be borne in mind that this was only the right flank-guard; our main attack, which was to be delivered against Sheria, was not timed to commence until two or three days later. However, the enemy elected to employ the whole of his available reserves in an immediate counter-attack. During the 4th and 5th he made several determined attacks on the mounted troops in this locality. These attacks were repulsed; and the enemy's action was not allowed to make any essential modification to the original plan, which it had been decided to carry out at dawn on November 6th. It was this exhausting of the Turkish reserves, so early in the operations and so far away to the East as Khuweilfeh, that paved the way for the success of our attack on Sheria.

At dawn, on the 6th, the force detailed for the main attack had taken up positions of readiness to the south-east of the Kauwukah system of trenches. The yeomanry opened the ball by assaulting the group of works forming the extreme left of the enemy's defensive system, following this up by an advance due west up the railway, capturing the line of detached works which lay east of the railway line. Meanwhile, London and Irish troops moved towards the Kauwukah system, bringing forward their guns to within wire-cutting range. Soon after noon, these troops commenced their attack upon the south-eastern face of the Kauwukah system. This was completely successful in capturing all its objectives. Sheria station was also reported as captured before dark. On this same day the right flank-guard, the 53rd Division, had successfully attacked Khuweilfeh. The position at nightfall, then, was that our right flank-guard were at Kauweilfeh, the yeomanry had reached the line of the Sheria to Wadi Union, and the troops on the left were close to Hareira Redoubt which was still occupied by the enemy.

Next day, the 7th, the situation remained practically unchanged on our extreme right, the enemy maintaining his positions opposite our right flank-guard. In the Sheria-Hareira locality, the Hareira Tepe Redoubt was captured at dawn. Tel el Sheria was captured at 4.0 a.m. and the line was pushed forward about a mile to the north of Tel el Sheria. That night the enemy withdrew.

Meanwhile, on our extreme left, the bombardment of Gaza had

continued. Another attack was ordered to take place on the night of the 6th/7th. An attack was made at 11.30 p.m. that night against Outpost Hill and Middlesex Hill, south of the town, which met with little opposition.

> As soon, after they had been taken, as patrols could be pushed forward, the enemy was found to be gone. Early in the morning, the main enemy force occupied the northern and eastern defences of Gaza. Rearguards were still occupying Beit Hanun and the Atawinah and Tank System (part of the Sihan group of works), from whence Turkish artillery continued to fire on Gaza and Ali Muntar until dusk.
>
> As soon as it was seen that the Turks had evacuated Gaza, on the morning of the 7th, a part of the force pushed along the coast to the mouth of the Wadi Hesi, some 8 miles north of Gaza, so as to turn the Wadi Hesi line and prevent the enemy making any stand there. This force reached the Wadi Hesi by evening, and succeeded in establishing itself on the north bank in the face of considerable opposition from a Turkish rearguard. Cavalry had already pushed on round the north of Gaza and become engaged at Beit Hanun with an enemy rearguard which maintained its position till nightfall.

This brings our history down to the night of November 7th/8th. By the morning of the 8th the enemy were in retreat all along the line.

Meanwhile, what had been happening to our own party in the Apex? The general plan of attack did not contemplate any advance from here. Nevertheless, it was necessary that this portion of the line should be firmly held, and it was more than likely that the enemy would try to create a diversion by raiding this inviting salient. By the end of October "liveliness" was increasing all round, and mutual bombardments were growing more intense. Fortunately, a large number of the shells fired by the enemy were "duds." We were puzzled at the time to know why duds figured so largely in this and following bombardments; subsequent inspection of the enemy trenches afforded an explanation. Great dumps of ammunition had been formed by the enemy close to the guns, and these, for safety and concealment, had been placed in deep dugouts.

On the evening of the 27th October, a great thunderstorm burst over Gaza, causing the enemy considerable damage, flooding the dugouts, and presumably damping the fuses and ruining their ammunition.

On the evening of the 3rd November, the enemy tried to create a diversion by raiding the Apex. On this evening we were sitting quietly having dinner in our headquarters dugout, when sharp rifle fire was heard from the front line of the battalion on our right. We walked out, and saw a veritable Brock's Benefit display of Verey lights. A telephone message from our front line informed us that a considerable party of the enemy had crept quietly up, and were now prowling round our wire and trying to pick a way through. A hot fire from rifles, Lewis guns and machine guns, soon convinced the enemy of the uselessness of attempting, without artillery preparation, a raid against an alert enemy well entrenched with wire intact. They were beaten off, and withdrew to a fold in the ground a couple of hundred yards out in No Man's Land, where they were fired upon by our trench mortars. Nevertheless they managed to rally, and came forward again to the attack.

This time their reception was no more encouraging than before; our artillery got into them with a barrage and they withdrew. Now they sent up a red Verey light signal, whereupon a hostile barrage came down upon our trenches, under cover of which they not only withdrew themselves, but also removed their killed and wounded. It is a part of their religion to spare no pains in removing their dead and giving them a decent burial. A couple of deserters crept into our lines towards the morning, from whom we were able to gather something about their side of the operations. Desertion was fairly common among the Turks about this time, partly because rations were poor, but mainly because they had no stomach for the fight that they knew to be imminent. In so far as this raid affected us, our trenches were badly smashed by the artillery, but our casualties were insignificant.

The next evening we sent a small patrol across No Man's Land, which, being boldly and pluckily led, crept right up to the enemy's trenches. Here they heard the sound of much traffic on the Gaza-Beersheba road, token doubtless of the impending withdrawal. More important from our immediate point of view, the patrol heard sounds of an enemy concentration in their front trenches, in apparent preparation for another raid on the Apex. Our artillery put salvoes at once upon those trenches; and the raid of that night proved a damp squib. About midnight we were wakened from our slumbers by a thunderstorm, the thunder, lightning and hail being provided by a deluge of bursting shells, splinters and shrapnel bullets. When the barrage lifted, glimpses were caught of the enemy moving along our front wire; but this raid never succeeded in forcing an entrance to our trenches.

We had every reason to "*remember the fifth of November.*" It came in with a display of fireworks; it went out like an inferno. Profiting by his previous experience, the enemy shelled a portion of our front deliberately from early evening until dark, with the obvious intention of cutting the wire on a portion of our sector. At ten o'clock that night, down came another intensive bombardment, which lasted for an hour. Under cover of the darkness, the enemy even brought trench mortars on camels up to our wire to assist in the bombardment. Next morning the ground looked like a veritable sea beach after a wreck; the litter consisted of splinters and duds of all sizes and descriptions, largely 5.9" H.Es.

This hostile barrage made a really satisfactory job of the wire cutting. As soon as it lifted, the enemy's infantry made a determined effort to penetrate our line. During the bombardment our fellows had taken shelter in the narrow passage ways behind the traverses, and so lost no time, immediately the barrage lifted, in manning the fire-step. They at once got busy with rifles, Lewis guns and machine-guns, and gave the Turk, as he crossed the ruins of our wire, a distinctly warm reception. This proved more than enough for most of the enemy; but a few brave spirits succeeded in entering our trench and throwing bombs. They were not supported by their fellows, and were soon disposed of. At length, up went the now familiar red light, down came the closing barrage, the enemy drew off and we were left in peace.

After these three abortive raids the Apex was left unmolested, except for occasional shelling on the 6th and 7th. On the 8th, we were relieved at the Apex by Lines of Communication troops, in order that we might take part in the pursuit of the enemy who were now in full retreat.

The quotations in this and the three following chapters, are from General Allenby's Despatch, dated the 16th December, 1917.

CHAPTER 8

Full Cry

We have seen that during the night of the 7th/8th November, the enemy had retreated all along the line. The enemy opposite our right flank-guard withdrew towards Hebron, that is, north-east into the Judaean Hills. He was pursued for a short distance by the yeomanry, and some prisoners and camels were captured. The yeomanry were then recalled to rejoin the main body of the mounted troops for the more important work of the pursuit of the enemy's main body. The enemy force that thus escaped into the hills there reorganized, and later descended to the plain on the flank of our pursuing force with a view to creating a diversion; but of this, more anon.

On the afternoon of the 7th, when it was seen that our Sheria operations in the centre had been successful, the cavalry were ordered to push forward from there in the direction of Huj, which was the terminus of the enemy's branch railway line from Deir Sineid. Had this force of cavalry been able to push forward and join up with the cavalry that had worked round by the sea and were engaging the enemy rearguard at Beit Hanun, the bulk of the Turkish force engaged upon this front might have been surrounded and captured. The mounted troops on the right moved towards Huj, but met with considerable opposition from hostile rearguards. On this account, and through difficulty in watering horses, the consummation devoutly to be desired was not attained.

It will be remembered that the Gaza operations had the effect of almost turning the enemy's right flank as long ago as November 2nd, and that, by the evening of the 7th, the force advancing along the coast had already established itself on the north bank of the Wadi Hesi, some 6 miles or so behind the enemy's defensive line.

Throughout the 7th, Turkish rearguards clung to Beit Hanun and to the Atawineh and Tank systems to the east of Ali Muntar. The effect of this was, that, when our troops eventually got under way in pursuit of the retreating Turks, those near the sea had several miles' start of those further inland. This feature, a pursuit in echelon with the left flank advanced, continued throughout these operations. And so we shall see that Jaffa fell into our hands some weeks before the capture of Jerusalem had even been attempted.

The bulk of the Turkish Army retreated northwards along the coastal plain. Here ran their railway, their main line of communications, and also an excellent road from Gaza to Jerusalem. Little or no opportunity was afforded of catching the disorganized enemy in narrow defiles, as happened in the rout of the following autumn, but the open plain offered ample opportunities for a hasty retreat, of which the enemy fully availed themselves.

> During the 8th, then, the advance was continued, and interest was chiefly centred in an attempt to cut off, if possible, the Turkish rearguard which had held the Tank and Atawineh systems. Considerable captures of prisoners, guns, ammunition and other stores were made, especially at Huj and Deir Sineid, but no large formed body of the enemy was cut off. The Turkish rearguards fought stubbornly and offered considerable opposition.

At this time the brunt of the work was being borne by the cavalry and the Royal Flying Corps, the infantry not having yet been ordered forward. "Near Huj, a fine charge by some squadrons of the Worcester and Warwick Yeomanry captured twelve guns, and broke the resistance of a hostile rearguard."

> It soon became obvious from the reports of the Royal Flying Corps, who throughout the 7th and 8th attacked the retreating columns with bombs and machine-gun fire, and from other evidence, that the enemy was retiring in considerable disorganization, and could offer no very serious resistance if pressed with determination.

> Instructions were accordingly issued on the morning of the 9th to the mounted troops, directing them on to the line El Tine-Beit Duras, that is, on to a line a little to the south-west of Junction Station, with orders to press the enemy relentlessly. A portion of the infantry was ordered forward in support.

> By the 9th, therefore, operations had reached the stage of a

direct pursuit by as many troops as could be supplied so far in front of the railhead.

The 54th Division had hitherto been principally engaged between Gaza and the sea. The 52nd Division, therefore, passed through the 54th and took up the pursuit along the coast, the pursuit along the Gaza-Jerusalem road falling to the lot of the 75th.

On the night of the 8th, our regiment was relieved in the trenches at the Apex, and, on the 9th, the 75th Division concentrated behind the line, ready to take its part in the pursuit. Next day we all went forward in column of route. We crossed No Man's Land along the enemy's old front line trenches by Ali Muntar. Having looked out upon this scene for months through glasses, telescopes and periscopes, it was interesting now to obtain a close view of these fortress defences.

But there were other sights that met our eyes, sad and gruesome, that can be better imagined than described. Portions of the enemy's wire, and of the gentle slopes in front, were littered with the remains of brave lads that had fallen in the sad days of March and April. It was strange that, in their own interests, the Turks had not buried these bodies. Instead they had left them lying there for months, beneath an almost tropical sun, and had actually fixed up their new wire entanglements over the unburied bodies. In some cases death had evidently been instantaneous. In others, where death had come more slowly, lads were to be found grasping open testaments or letters from home. It seemed so sad that these poor fellows, who had endured the hardships of the desert and marched victoriously across Sinai, should, like Moses, have been privileged to see, but not to enter, the Promised Land.

After crossing No Man's Land, we marched along past pleasanter sights, great stacks of ammunition, gas cylinders, and other interesting captures. We enjoyed glimpses of how the enemy here had made himself comfortable; still more did we enjoy glimpses of how we here had made the enemy uncomfortable. Huge craters there were, made by naval guns shelling from the sea. These guns had bombarded the enemy communications behind his front line, and had obtained direct hits on the track and rolling stock, causing a train or two, valuable booty, to fall into our possession. Bomb holes were to be seen, made by our aircraft in their efforts to destroy the bridges on the enemy's line of retreat.

We bivouacked on the night of the 10th at Deir Sineid. For the next two days we marched forward, close upon the heels of the pursuing cavalry, but not close enough yet to come into action or to deploy from column of route. All along our route lay evidences of the enemy's rout. At one time, we were passing a convoy of prisoners being shepherded along by a few cavalry; at another, a party of refugees hurrying back with their worldly possessions to those homes to which they knew they could now return in safety. Here and there lay the body of some unfortunate Turk; while all along the line lay the wreckage of vehicles and the carcases of transport animals.

Throughout these days the troops suffered considerably from thirst. A hot exhausting wind was blowing, and the men were heavily laden for long-distance route marching in a semi-tropical country. Water was the ever-recurring trouble. A little for the men to carry on with was generally procurable, but the difficulty of watering the animals at times became acute. The usual tidings were, that there was plenty of water at the next village. When the next village was reached the tidings proved to be true, but so long was the queue of animals already waiting to be watered, that fresh arrivals stood but little chance. At many places the water was insufficient; and:

> . . . . even when water was found in sufficient quantities, it was usually in wells and not on the surface; consequently, if the machinery for working the wells was damaged, or a sufficient supply of troughs was not available, the process of watering a large quantity of animals was slow and difficult.

Meanwhile, how were our cavalry progressing? A glance at the map will show that, after the fall of Gaza, the next point of tactical importance in Palestine was Junction Station. With this in our hands, Jerusalem would be cut off from railway communication with the outer world, and quantities of rolling stock, supplies, war material and possibly prisoners, should fall into our hands. While still pursuing the retreating enemy, therefore, the cavalry had been directed to make Junction Station their next objective.

The portion of the enemy's force that had withdrawn into the hills towards Hebron now made a descent from the hills to the plain. Their object was to threaten the flank of our pursuing cavalry, create a diversion, and thus relieve the pressure from their main body. From Hebron, a couple of difficult tracks wind down the mountains to the village of Beit Jibrin, where they join a road coming from Bethlehem and Jerusalem. This latter road reaches the plain and Beersheba railway at Arak el Menshiyeh. This was the spot, then, towards which the counter-attack, or demonstration from the hills, was organized.

It was obvious that the Hebron force, which was believed to be short of transport and ammunition, to have lost heavily, and to be in a generally disorganized state, could make no effective diversion, and that this threat could practically be disregarded. The Imperial Camel Corps, however, was ordered to move to the neighbourhood of Tel el Nejile, where it would be on the flank of any counterstroke from the hills; while orders were issued for the main pursuit to be pressed so that Junction Station might be reached with all speed. The Hebron group made an ineffective demonstration in the direction of Arak el Menshiyeh on the 10th, and then retired north-east so as to prolong the enemy's line towards Beit Jibrin.

Close to the sea, the advance-guard of the 52nd Division pushed on as far as Burkah on the 11th, and, on the 12th, the yeomanry pushed north and seized Tel el Murreh, on the right or northern bank of the Nahr Sukereir and close to its mouth.

"The operations of these days showed a stiffening of the enemy's resistance on the general line of the Wadi Sukereir, with centre about El Kustineh. Reports from the R.F.C. indicated the total hostile forces opposed to us on this line at about 15,000; and this increased resistance, coupled with the capture of prisoners from almost every unit of the Turkish force, tended to show that we were no longer opposed to rearguards, but that all the remainder of the Turkish Army, which could be induced to fight, was making a last effort to arrest our pursuit south of the important Junction Station.

"On the morning of the 13th November, the situation was, that the enemy had strung out his force on a front of 20 miles from El Kubeibeh on the north to about Beit Jibrin to the south. The right half of his line ran roughly parallel to, and only about five miles in front of, the railway to the north of Junction Station, which was the main line of supply from the north."

We have seen that our pursuit along the sea coast had a considerable start of that further to the right, and the rapidity of this pursuit had dictated to the enemy this rather unsatisfactory position which he was forced to take up. His right flank was already almost turned. In so far as he could do so, he held a strong position on the line of heights running north and south near the right flank of his position, on which heights stand the villages of Katrah and El Mughar.

The 12th was a day of preparation. On the 13th, an attack was delivered against the enemy's position by the 75th Division on the right and the 52nd on the left, the extreme right of the attack being protected by the Australian Mounted Troops, who had pressed forward towards Balin Berkussie and Tel es Safi. The country over which the attack took place is open and rolling. It is dotted with small villages surrounded by mud walls, with plantations of trees and thick cactus hedges outside the walls. These hedges afforded admirable opportunities for the concealment of machine guns. In spite of heavy machine gun fire, the 75th attacked and captured the village of El Mesmiye. A turning movement was directed against the enemy's right flank. There was a dashing charge of mounted troops, who galloped across the plain under heavy fire and turned the enemy's position from the north. The Kahan El Mughar position, protecting the enemy's right flank, fell to the 52nd Division. After this, the enemy resistance weakened, and by the evening his forces were in retreat. Early the following morning we occupied Junction Station.

The enemy's flight from Junction Station was precipitate. Two trains escaped shortly before our occupation, one of which was believed to have contained Von Kressenstein himself. Nevertheless our captures of rolling stock and material were considerable. The enemy's army had now been broken into two separate parts, which retired eastwards towards Jerusalem and northwards through Ramleh towards Tul Keram.

Throughout the 14th our mounted troops pressed on toward Ramleh and Ludd. On the right, Naaneh, on the railway to Ramleh, was attacked and captured in the morning. On the left, the New Zealand Mounted Rifles had a smart engagement at Ayun Kara, 6 miles south of Jaffa, where the Turks made a determined counter-attack, and were only repulsed at the point of the bayonet.

On the morning of the 15th our mounted troops dislodged a hostile rearguard, which had taken up a position on the high ground, flanking the railway north of Junction Station, and covering the main road from Jaffa to Jerusalem. This is the site of Gezer, one of the most ancient of the Canaanitish cities in Palestine, and one of the first objects of interest sought by the eye of the tourist on his journey up from Jaffa to Jerusalem. Thus, commanding both the railway and the main Jerusalem road, this position might have considerably delayed our advance had it been held with determination. As it was, our mounted troops were able to occupy Ramleh and Ludd that evening and to push forward patrols to within a short distance of Jaffa.

Jaffa, the ancient port of Jerusalem, was occupied without further opposition on the evening of the 16th.

> The situation was now as follows. The enemy's army, cut in two by our capture of Junction Station, had retired partly east into the mountains towards Jerusalem, and partly north along the Plain. The nearest line on which these two portions could reunite was the line Tul Keram–Nablus." Although Jerusalem itself could still be supplied along the road connecting it with Nablus, or along the road across the Jordan to Ammam Station on the Hejaz Railway, yet reports from the R.F.C. indicated that it was the probable intention of the enemy to evacuate Jerusalem and withdraw to organize on the line Tul Keram–Nablus.
>
> On our side, the mounted troops had been marching and fighting continuously since October 31st, and had advanced a distance of 75 miles measured in a straight line from Asluj to Jaffa. The infantry, after their last fighting at Gaza, had advanced, in nine days, distances of from 40 to 70 miles, with two severe engagements and continual advanced-guard fighting. The railway was being pushed forward as rapidly as possible, and every opportunity was taken of landing stores at points along the coast; but the landing of stores was dependent on a continuance of favourable weather, and might at any moment be stopped for several days together.
>
> A pause was therefore necessary to await the progress of railway construction. But before our position in the plain could be considered secure, it was essential to push forward into the hills, and to obtain a hold of the one good road which traverses the Judaean range from north to south, from Nablus to Jerusalem.

CHAPTER 9

Neby Samwil

Our advance had hitherto been northwards along the low country, and had already reached a point on the Maritime Plain some miles north of the parallel of Jerusalem. It now wheeled to the right and struck into the Hills, with the object of getting astride the Jerusalem-Nablus road and of thus capturing the Holy City.

It will be remembered, from our survey of the geography of Palestine, that the ridge of the Judaean Hills runs approximately north and south, and that along the top of this ridge runs a first-class metalled road connecting Nablus with Jerusalem. From this ridge spurs run east and west down towards the Maritime Plain. These spurs are steep, bare and stony, and in places, precipitous, and are separated from one another by narrow valleys. Between such spurs, a few miles to the north-west of Jerusalem, sweeps down the Valley of Ajalon, with the villages of Beit-ur el-Foka (Beth-horon the Upper) and Beit-ur el-Tahta (Beth-horon the Lower), where Joshua won his memorable victory over the five kings of the Amorites.

It was here that the routed hosts of the Amorites were pursued in panic, and near here that the sun and moon "stood still" at the bidding of Joshua. Further to the south, another gorge, or pass, roughly parallel to the Valley of Ajalon, leads down to the plain, and along this pass runs the metalled road through Kurzet-el-Enab (Kirjath-Jearim), Saris and Bab-el-Wad, to Ramleh and Jaffa; this is the road followed by the Pilgrims. Other paths were shown upon the map, but these were found to be mere tracks on the hillside or up the stony beds of *wadis*, and, without considerable improvement, were impracticable for wheeled guns or transport. The only routes along which guns, other than mountain artillery, could be moved, were the two first-class roads running northwards and westwards out of Jerusalem.

Ten miles north of Jerusalem, along the Nablus road, at a height of nearly 3,000 feet above sea level, is the village of Bireh. This commanding position overlooks the Jordan Valley and all the surrounding country. This was the point which General Allenby decided to make his next objective. Reports had indicated that it was the probable intention of the enemy to evacuate Jerusalem, and in the known or suspected state of the demoralisation of the enemy, it was felt that considerable risks could be taken. Thus a bold and immediate dash for Bireh seemed to be indicated. Furthermore, an advance on this objective would take our forces well clear of Jerusalem itself. And so this plan best conformed with the determination that had previously been arrived at, that fighting should be within five miles of the Holy City.

The general idea of the operation was, that our troops should move up into the hills, some going by the Valley of Ajalon, and some by the main Jaffa-Jerusalem road as far as Enab, and thence by the "Roman road" running north-east. Although it was thought likely that the Turks, reinforced from Damascus, and perhaps from Aleppo, would come down and attack our new line, yet it was hoped that Bireh would be reached before serious opposition was encountered. The enemy, however, changed his mind. Having, early in November, decided to withdraw from Jerusalem, he now determined to hold it till the bitter end. Turkish resistance stiffened immensely. Pushed far into the hills, as were our advanced troops, and without much artillery support, it was found impossible for them to reach Bireh in the first stride; and further operations upon a more elaborate scale had to be undertaken before Jerusalem could be captured.

But we anticipate. Let us, then, return to the middle of November, at which time our forces had captured, and were holding, positions covering Jaffa, Ramleh and Junction Station. On the 17th November, the yeomanry commenced to move from Ramleh through the hills direct on Bireh, *via* the valley of Ajalon and Lower Beth-horon; and, by the evening of the 18th, one portion of the yeomanry had reached Lower Beth-horon, while another portion had occupied Shilta.

On the 19th, the infantry commenced its advance. Latron and An-was were captured in the morning. For nearly 4 miles, between Bab el Wad (2½ miles east of Latron) and Saris, the Jaffa-Jerusalem road passes through a narrow gorge or defile. The remainder of the day was spent in clearing this defile up to Saris. "These narrow passes from the plain to the plateau of the Judaean range have seldom been forced, and have been fatal to many invading armies." The natural facilities for

71

defence in this pass were undoubtedly very strong. "Had the attempt not been made at once, or had it been pressed with less determination, the enemy would have had time to reorganize his defences here, and the conquest of the plateau would then have been slow, costly and precarious."

The character of the fighting now changed, and more nearly resembled the mountain warfare of the north-west frontier of India. The bulk of this hill fighting fell upon the 75th Division, whose Indian experience proved invaluable. It was interesting to note the points of resemblance and of distinction between hill fighting here and on the Indian frontier.

In India, frontier warfare is usually conducted against ill-organized semi-savages, unarmed with artillery or machine guns, but furnished with the instincts and cunning of beasts of prey. Here the conditions were reversed. The enemy were well provided with artillery and machine guns, both of which they had had abundant opportunity to post advantageously and use effectually; whereas we had difficulties in getting forward our guns and bringing them into action, and were at times without artillery assistance. On the other hand, our troops surpassed the enemy in their familiarity with mountain fighting.

Here, as in all mountain fighting, the cardinal principle was piquetting the heights—that is to say, the necessity of sending up piquets from the advanced-guard, who deny to the enemy all commanding eminences, before the main body and transport move up the defile which those eminences command. Our piquets had frequently to fight their way up to the heights, and to be prepared, on reaching the summit, to withstand a shelling or repulse a counter-attack. They had, therefore, to be stronger than is usually necessary in India, but had to be particularly careful not to concentrate too much upon the summit. In India, where the enemy generally fight a guerilla warfare, hanging on to rearguards and cutting off stragglers, the stiffest part of the fighting is to be expected during the subsequent withdrawal of the piquets from the heights.

Here, the fighting was done by the advanced-guard, and during the taking of the heights, subsequent withdrawal being generally unmolested. Quickness in the attack was found to be of great value. In some cases the garrisons of heights were surprised and captured before they could get away; more than once the advanced-guard, pushing rapidly up the road, were able to cut off such garrisons as they were coming down the reverse slopes of their hills.

With regard to armament, our field artillery were able to assist with their 4.2 inch howitzers, but the 18-pounder field guns, with their flat projectory, were, at this stage, found to be of little use. During later stages of this mountain warfare, the 18-pounder came again into its own; but that was when suitable positions could be chosen deliberately, and when, through the length of the range or the use of reduced charges, they were able to drop their shells with a steep angle of descent. A high velocity gun, with a flat projectory, like our 18-pounder, has two disadvantages in mountain warfare. When the gun is firing from behind a steep hill, the shell, on leaving the gun, is liable to strike the hill in front instead of clearing the crest.

When the projectile reaches the distant ridge (behind which the enemy are presumably taking cover), the angle of descent is not sufficiently steep to cause damage. More satisfactory results were obtainable with howitzers, whose high angle fire could both clear the forward crests and search the reverse slopes. Unfortunately, at this time, we had little or no mountain artillery up forward, while the wheeled guns were often badly handicapped for want of good roads. We had marched away from Gaza well enough supplied with artillery for normal or plain country fighting, but scarcely so for this very different fighting in the mountains.

Another disadvantage under which we laboured, through this abrupt merging from trench into mountain warfare, was the overloading of the men. For the latter class of warfare men must be lightly equipped; in India, even the men's great-coats are carried for them on pack-mules. Here, the men were, of necessity, loaded up as for trench fighting, and were carrying gas masks and extra bandoliers (50 rounds) of ammunition, making a total of 170 rounds per man.

The key to success in modern mountain fighting proved to be the rapidity with which roads could be constructed for bringing forward artillery.

The defile up to Saris having been piquetted and cleared on the 19th, Enab was captured on the 20th in the face of organized opposition. Other infantry had moved from the plain along the more northern track (the Ajalon Valley route) by Berfilja and Beit Likia, and, on this same 20th, they captured Beit Dukka. On the same day the yeomanry got to within 4 miles of the Nablus-Jerusalem road, but were stopped by strong opposition about Beihesnia, 3 or 4 miles west-south-west of Bireh.

In this night it rained, as only in tropical and semi-tropical countries it knows how. The men, clad in their Indian drill, were soaked immediately, and lay down on the road or in the streets of Enab, or slept where they stood, the picture of misery. An isolated Turk rushed down the road, determined to sell his life dearly. But he could find nobody enthusiastic enough to fight, or even to take sufficient interest in him to accept his surrender; until at last he found a military policeman, who, this being his job, had no alternative but to take him prisoner. At length dawn broke; and it then became clear that Enab was under Turkish observation. So a cold night of rain was followed by a hot morn of fire.

From Enab, a "Roman road" leaves the main Jaffa-Jerusalem road and strikes away north-east to Biddu, and thence towards Bireh. In Roman days, this may have been an important road, but now it was found to be a mere rocky track, impassable for wheels, or for anything except infantry and pack animals. On the morning of the 21st, a portion of the 75th Division moved forward by this track, while another portion of the Division was left at Enab to cover the flank and demonstrate along the main Jerusalem road.

The latter body drove hostile parties from Kushel, 2½ miles east of Enab, and secured this ridge. Meanwhile, progress along the "Roman road" was slow. The track was under hostile shell-fire, and it was found impossible to bring up guns to support the advance of the infantry. The advanced guard, pushing on towards Bireh, had got as far as Biddu, when it was held up there by intensive hostile shelling. The remainder of the leading brigade thereupon captured a commanding position about a couple of miles to the east of Biddu, and 2½ miles short of the Jerusalem-Nablus road. This commanding position was Neby Samwil.

Neby Samwil, one of the most prominent heights round Jerusalem, must always have been a place of considerable importance. It is identified with Mizpeh, one of the cities built by King Asa. Ecclesiastical tradition connects this place with Ramah, the birth and burial place of the prophet Samuel, whose tomb is said to lie under the Crusading Church, the ruins of which still exist here. To the honour of this prophet, the Moslems had erected a fine mosque upon this spot, which was a landmark for miles round. As subsequent events proved, Neby Samwil was the key to Jerusalem.

The question has been often asked: Who was the first to capture Neby Samwil? The honour has sometimes been claimed for the 60th Division. No doubt that division fought here, and fought well. But at least two other divisions, the 52nd and the 75th, had been fighting on this hill for a day or so before the arrival of the 60th. As a matter of fact, this hill, the "key" to Jerusalem, was first captured by a brigade of the 75th Division, in honour of which a "key" was thereafter adopted as the proud distinguishing mark of this division.

On Neby Samwil occurred some of the bitterest fighting in the Palestine campaign. Both sides realized the vital importance of the position. All the first night the hill was distinctly unhealthy. The trees were infested with snipers who picked off our men in the bright moonlight. Some refuge from the sniping was procurable inside the Mosque, but the Turkish artillery had no compunction in shelling the building and bringing it down in ruins. As the night progressed, more troops were poured on to the hill. The snipers were hunted down and summarily dealt with. Machine guns were established in the ruined Mosque and other appropriate positions, and preparations made to hold the hill at all costs.

Towards the morning the Turks delivered a determined counter-attack. During the 22nd, the enemy made two counter-attacks on the Neby Samwil Ridge, which we repulsed. In one case, the Ghurkhas, having run out of ammunition, hurled down rocks and boulders upon the heads of the ascending enemy. At one time the Mosque was deserted by all except one machine-gun officer, who continued to work his gun single-handed. By this time the 52nd Division had come up and were, in some cases relieving, in some fighting side by side with, the 75th.

On the 23rd and on the 24th, determined and gallant attacks were made on the strong positions to the west of the Nablus road held by the enemy, who had brought up reinforcements and numerous machine guns, and could support his infantry by artillery fire from guns placed in position along the main road. Our artillery, from lack of roads, could not be brought up to give adequate support to our infantry, and both attacks failed. The yeomanry, who by the afternoon of the 21st had got to within a couple of miles of the Nablus road, were heavily counter-attacked, and fell back, after bitter fighting, on Beit-ur el-Foka (Upper Beth-horon).

This fighting had been taking place over classical and sacred ground. Troops fighting on Neby Samwil looked down upon the Holy City, still in the hands of the Turk. Our advanced dressing station was established in the beautiful monastery on the traditional site of Emmaus; here the men were dying on the very spot that the risen Christ had

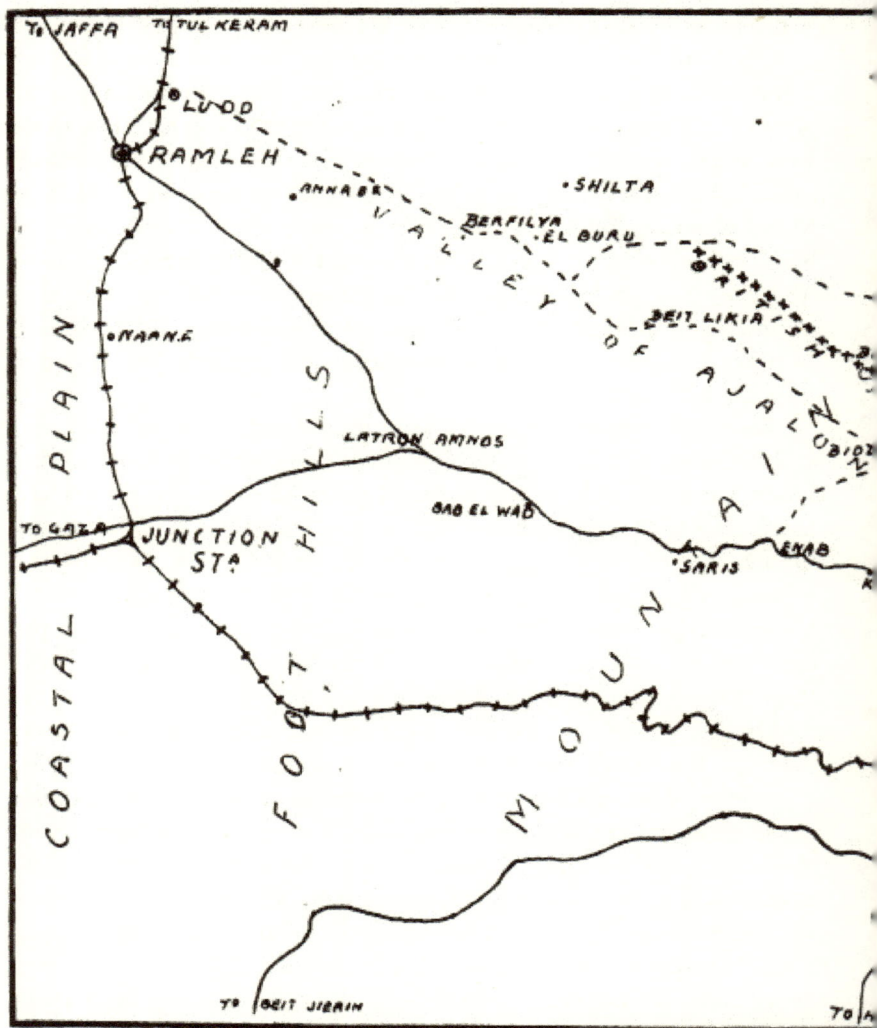

TO JAFFA   TO TUL KERAM

LUDD

RAMLEH

SHILTA

ANNA BE

VALLEY   BERFILYA
EL BURJ

NAANE   BEIT LIKIA   OBIN

PLAIN

LATRON AMNOS   OF

BAB EL WAD   AJALON

TO GAZA   JUNCTION   SARIS   ENAB
STA.

FOOT HILLS

COASTAL   MOUN

TO BEIT JIBRIN   TO

TO NABLUS

BEITIN

HRI ALLB   BIREH

UNIA

MUKKMAS

TO R.JORDAN
ES SALT &
AMMAN
JERICHO

UKKA

BEIT IZZA

NEBI SAMWIL

BEIT IKSA

1917

JERUSALEM
MOUNT OF
OLIVES

JORDAN VALLEY

BEIT SURAFAT

BETHLEHEM

SKETCH MAP
OF
COUNTRY ROUND JERUSALEM
ILLUSTRATING THE OPERATIONS FOR
THE CAPTURE OF THE CITY

MILES 0   1   2   3   4   5   10

DEAD
SEA

RON

been made known to His disciples in the breaking of bread.

The positions reached on the evening of the 21st practically marked the limit of the progress in this first attempt to gain the Nablus road. Positions had been won from which our final attack could be prepared and delivered with good prospects of success. Nevertheless, it was evident that a period of preparation and organization would be necessary before an attack could be delivered in sufficient strength to drive the enemy from his positions.

Orders were accordingly issued to consolidate the position gained and prepare for relief. The 60th Division had been lent to the 21st Corps, and had already taken their place in the fighting on Neby Samwil. Now the 21st Corps were gradually relieved and moved over to the left; while the operations about Jerusalem were taken over by the 20th Corps.

CHAPTER 10

Jerusalem

Let us trace the fortunes of the 20th Corps, whom we last saw engaged in the fighting about Beersheba. After the fall of Gaza and Beersheba, most of the mounted troops went forward in pursuit of the enemy along the Maritime Plain. These were closely followed up and supported by the 21st Corps, *i.e.* the 52nd and 75th Divisions, with the 54th following close upon their heels. It was impossible at this time to supply more than a limited number of troops far forward of railhead. So the Divisions of the 20th Corps after their successful operations at Beersheba and Sheria, were first moved backwards to rest and re-equip, before going forward again into the field zone. Of these 20th Corps Divisions, the 60th were the first to go forward. Following along the main Gaza-Junction Station road, in the footsteps of the 75th and 54th Divisions, the 60th arrived at Junction Station on the 22nd November, on which date the headquarters of the 20th Corps also moved up to, and opened at, Junction Station.

The 60th Division were now lent to the 21st Corps. They moved forward next day, following along the Jerusalem road to Enab, and about the 24th or 25th began to take their place in the fighting on the Neby Samwil ridge. Shortly after the 60th came forward the 74th. By the time that they got sufficiently far forward, the 20th Corps were taking over from, and relieving, the 21st, and the 74th Division soon found itself in the zone of operations to the west and north-west of Jerusalem. The 10th Division remained in the neighbourhood of Gaza for a few weeks, until the possibilities of supply permitted their also going forward. The 53rd Division did not go forward by the Maritime Plain at all. They remained about Beersheba until the 4th December. Then they moved forward, without meeting with opposition, along the higher road, that is, through Hebron towards Bethlehem; and subsequently arrived in the hills at such time and place as their presence was required for manoeuvring the enemy out of Jerusalem.

While these reliefs were in progress, several determined counter-attacks were delivered by the enemy in their attempt to dislodge us from the positions of advantage that we had already gained. At this time our line was, of necessity, somewhat thinly held, especially towards the sea. The Imperial Camel Corps, whom we last saw protecting the right flank of the pursuit from the threat near Beit Jibrin, had been moved across to the extreme left, where they and cavalry held positions on the north bank of the River Auja, protecting Jaffa. Further to the right, the line was carried on by the 54th Division, who thus linked up, along the ridge north of the Valley of Ajalon, with the 52nd and 75th Divisions then fighting in the neighbourhood of Neby Samwil.

> On the 25th November our advanced posts north of the River Auja were driven back across the river. An attack on the night of the 29th succeeded in penetrating our outpost line northeast of Jaffa; but next morning the whole hostile detachment, numbering 150, was surrounded and captured by the Australian Light Horse. Attacks were also delivered against the left flank of our position in the hills from Beit-ur el-Foka to El Burj and the Neby Samwil ridge. One such attack was delivered on the 30th near El Burj, when a counter-attack by Australian Light Horse took 200 prisoners and practically destroyed the attacking battalion. There was particularly heavy fighting between El Burj and Beit-ur el-Foka, but all these attacks were successfully resisted and severe losses were inflicted on the enemy. All efforts by the enemy to drive us off the Neby Samwil ridge were completely repulsed.

> These attacks in no way affected our positions nor impeded the progress of our preparations. Favoured by a continuance of fine weather, preparations for a fresh advance against the Turkish positions west and south of Jerusalem proceeded rapidly. Existing roads and tracks were improved and new ones constructed to enable heavy and field artillery to be placed in position and ammunition and supplies brought up. The water supply was also developed. By December 4th all reliefs were complete.

A line was then held from Kushel, about 5 miles to the west of Jerusalem, along the ridge that runs north-east some 3 or 4 miles to

Neby Samwil. From this point, the line bent back at a right angle, and ran along the northern ridge of the Valley of Ajalon through Beit Izza and Beit Dukka to Beit-ur el-Tahta (Beth-horon the Lower), from which point it was carried west and north-west to the sea.

The enemy held a line approximately facing our Kushel-Neby Samwil line, protecting Jerusalem from attack from the west or north-west, his front line being distant about three miles from the city, and artillery and machine guns being posted in the outskirts of the city itself. He had two good lines of supply or retreat, namely the north road from Nablus and the eastern road through Jericho and across the Jordan to Amman Station on the Hejaz Railway. It will be remembered that, in the words of the Psalmist, "The Hills stand round about Jerusalem." The Turks were able to select positions of considerable natural strength in these surrounding hills. In fact, the country is one continual succession of hills and valleys, the hillsides steep and rocky, the valleys deep and strewn with boulders. These positions of natural strength the enemy had improved by the construction of trenches and strong points and other devices of modern field engineering.

The general idea of the operations for the capture of Jerusalem was the simultaneous pressure of three Divisions, whereby the enemy should be driven off his main roads, and the city be isolated, and so forced to surrender. The 60th and 74th Divisions had already arrived in the fighting zone and were occupying positions in the line, the 60th on the right, about Kushel, and the 74th about Neby Samwil. On December 4th, the 53rd Division commenced their march from Beersheba up the Hebron-Jerusalem Road. No opposition was met, and, by the evening of the 6th, the head of this column was ten miles north of Hebron. The infantry were directed to reach the Bethlehem area by the 7th, and a line about three miles south of Jerusalem by dawn on the 8th. The 8th was the date fixed for the commencement of the renewed operations against Jerusalem.

On the 7th the weather broke, and for three days rain was almost continuous. The hills were covered with mist at frequent intervals throughout the fighting, rendering observation from the air and visual signalling impossible.

Great was the discomfort caused to the men by this rain, fog and mud. The cold was intense, and soldiers who had borne the brunt of a long day's fighting could not sleep, but just lay huddled together longing for the dawn. An even more serious effect of the rain was to jeopardise the supply arrangements, by converting the roads into seas of liquid mud, rendering them almost impassable, in places quite impassable for camels and mechanical transport.

By dawn on the 8th, all the troops were in their allotted positions, except the 53rd Division. It had been recognized that these troops on the extreme right might be delayed and fail to reach the positions assigned to them by dawn on the 8th, and arrangements had accordingly been made for the protection of our right flank west of Jerusalem in case of such delay occurring. This contingency did occur. The 53rd Division was held up by mud and fog, and by roads blown up by the enemy, so that, by the morning of the 8th, it was still some distance south of Jerusalem; on that day it exercised little or no influence on the fighting.

During the darkness of the night of the 7th/8th December, and in weather such as we have described, portions of the 60th Division clambered down the mountain side, crossed the deep *wadi* bed in front of the right of our line, and crept up the steep terraced sides of the opposite ridge where ran a portion of the Turkish line. One brigade was to make a frontal attack, while another was to turn the left flank of the enemy's position, by scaling a spur to the south-west of the village of Ain Karim. These two brigades stormed the main line of works before daylight and captured the western defences of Jerusalem. Considerable rifle and artillery fire was experienced from the outskirts of Jerusalem, so that it was necessary for our troops to throw back their right and form a defensive flank facing eastwards towards the city.

Artillery support from our own guns soon became difficult, owing to the length of the advance and the difficulty of moving guns forward. It thus became difficult for these troops to attain their subsequent objectives in the direction of the Nablus road north of Jerusalem. Accordingly, it was decided, early in the afternoon, to consolidate the line gained and resume the advance next day, when the right column (the 53rd Division) would be in a position to exert its pressure.

Meanwhile, the task of the 74th Division was to swing forward, with their left resting and pivoting on Neby Samwil, to capture Beit Iksa village and works, and so to swing forward to the Nablus road. They each captured their first objective, and we were preparing for a further advance. But the delay on the right made it desirable to check for the time the advance on the left, and to consolidate the positions already attained.

By nightfall, our line ran from Neby Samwil to the east of Beit

Iksa, through Lifta, to a point of about 1½ miles west of Jerusalem, whence it was thrown back facing east. Thus, our main line had swung forward, circling on its pivot at Neby Samwil, with its extreme right flank refused. The refused right flank afforded protection against the fire coming from the city. The main directions of our advance, however, now menaced, not so much Jerusalem itself, as the main Nablus road a few miles to the north of the city. All the enemy's prepared defences west and north-west of Jerusalem had been captured, and our troops were within a short distance of the Nablus-Jerusalem Road.

That night the Turks withdrew. On the following morning, the 9th December, the 74th and 60th Divisions, driving back rearguards, occupied a line across the Nablus-Jerusalem road 4 miles north of Jerusalem.

In the meantime, the 53rd Division had arrived on the scene of operations to the south of Jerusalem. They bore right-handed, cleared the Mount of Olives, which commands Jerusalem from the east, drove the enemy away eastwards, and occupied a position east of Jerusalem across the Jericho road.

These operations isolated Jerusalem. At about noon on the 9th December, 1918, the city was surrendered.

Two days later General Allenby made his official entry into Jerusalem. It was a simple ceremony. The general entered the city on foot, preceded by his *aides-de-camp*, and accompanied by the commanders of the French and Italian detachments, by the French, Italian and American military *attachés*, and by a few members of the general staff. Outside the Jaffa Gate he was received by the military governor, and a guard of honour composed of representatives of troops from the various portions of the British Empire, which had taken part in the recent operations; while, inside the walls, were small parties from the French and Italian detachments which those countries had sent to assist us in Palestine.

Inside the city, at the base of the Tower of David, the ceremony was concluded by the reading of the proclamation. Its terms promised that every person could pursue his lawful business without interruption, and that every sacred building, monument, holy spot, shrine, traditional site, endowment, pious bequest, or customary place of prayer of whatsoever form of the great religions of mankind, would be maintained and protected according to the existing customs and beliefs of those to whose faiths they were sacred.

CHAPTER 11

The Holy City

[1]It is beyond the scope of this book to attempt a detailed history of Jerusalem. It cannot, however, fail to interest those readers who have followed us thus far, if we glance at a few incidents in the history of this sacred spot.

Of little importance, perhaps non-existent, in the days of the Patriarchs, and still in the hands of the Jebusites through the days of Joshua, the Judges, and Samuel, it first sprang into fame about a thousand years before Christ when it was captured by King David, who made it his capital. Solomon built his temple on Mount Moriah, and prayed to Jehovah that He would especially hear the prayers of His people when they prayed toward the city which He had chosen and the House which Solomon had built for His name. Then did this city become, and has ever since remained, the sacred city of the Jews.

With the advent of Christ, born within a few miles of its walls, Who here preached and healed, instituted His Holy Sacrament, suffered under Pontius Pilate, was crucified, dead and buried and the third day rose again from the dead, Who here laid the foundations of the most beautiful religion that the world has ever seen, Jerusalem became and has ever since remained, the sacred city of the Christian.

And then, six hundred years later, came the rise of Islam. The great prophet Mahomet, in evolving his religion, based his teaching upon the principles of Judaism and Christianity, the prophets of which were to be honoured, including "the prophet David" and "the Prophet Christ." So, in accordance with the prayer of Solomon, and until the antagonism between Judaism and Islam led to the substitution of

---

1. Much of the material in this chapter is derived from Milman's *History of the Jews*, W. Besant and E. H. Palmer's *Jerusalem*, and George Adam Smith's *Historical Geography of the Holy Land*, to which my acknowledgments are accordingly due.

Mecca, it was towards Jerusalem that devout Moslems were required to turn when they prayed. From Mount Moriah did Mahomet, as his followers believe, miraculously ascend to heaven. And so did Jerusalem become, and has ever since remained, no less a sacred city of the Mahomedan.

Thus it will be seen that Jerusalem, the sacred city of three mighty religions, became the most holy city in the world, the poetical prototype of heaven.

Jerusalem, situate away on the hills and far from the main trading and military route, was of but little commercial or strategical importance. Yet we readily understand how its religious value caused it so often to become the goal and prize of contending creeds and armies. Sometimes the motive was religious antagonism, as with Antiochus Epiphanes and Titus; sometimes it was religious devotion, as with the Maccabees and Crusaders. Pitiful though it be, yet, throughout the ages, the City of the Prince of Peace has been associated with the most terrible scenes, the most savage excesses, in the whole dreadful drama of war.

Not once nor twice in the reigns of the Kings of Judah and Israel, did Jerusalem resound with the clash of arms. Although, after the fall of the northern kingdom, it was delivered by divine intervention from the invasion of Sennacherib, yet its submersion by the rising tide of Babylon could not long be averted. The evil day had only been postponed and, in 607 B.C., Jerusalem fell before Nebuchadnezzar, before that power which, like Turkey of yesterday, dominated the whole stretch of country from the Persian Gulf to the border of Egypt. Twenty years later, Jerusalem, with the Temple of Solomon, was destroyed, the city, palaces and temple being levelled in one, and the population were put to death or led away captive to Babylon.

When, some years later, the capital of the Babylonians was captured by the Persians and their empire annexed, the Jews were permitted to return to Jerusalem. In the sixth and fifth centuries b.c. the temple and walls were rebuilt under Ezra and Nehemiah, and Jerusalem took a fresh lease of life as a Jewish city.

In the fourth century B.C., when Alexander the Great marched southwards through Syria to Egypt, securing the Mediterranean littoral before embarking on his expedition into Asia, overthrowing Tyre in his march and totally destroying Gaza, the Jews no doubt made their submission, and their city thus escaped destruction.

After the death of Alexander, Judaea did not escape the anarchy which ensued during the internecine warfare waged by his generals and successors. In 321 B.C., Ptolemy I, King of Egypt, advanced against Jerusalem, and, assaulting it on the Sabbath, the Jew's day of rest, met with no resistance. He is said to have carried away 100,000 captives, whom he settled in Alexandria and Cyrene. The founding of a Syro-Grecian kingdom in Northern Syria brought Judaea again into the unfortunate situation of a buffer state. Jerusalem seemed doomed to be among the prizes of an interminable warfare between the Ptolemies of Egypt and the Seleucidæ of Syria and in turns vassal to each.

At the commencement of the second century B.C. Judaea passed into the hands of the Syrian King Antiochus the Great, who at once proceeded to ingratiate himself with the whole nation. It was not the tyranny of foreign sovereigns, but the unprincipled ambition of their own native rulers, that led to calamities little less dreadful than the Babylonian captivity. Jason, the High Priest, had been dispossessed by his brother Menelaus, by double dealing with the Syrian king, who at this time was Antiochus Epiphanes. A rumour of the king's death having reached Palestine in 170 B.C., Jason seized the opportunity and revolted against his brother Menelaus. But the rumour was false.

> The intelligence of the insurrection, magnified into a deliberate revolt of the whole nation, reached Antiochus. He marched without delay against Jerusalem, put to death in three days' time 40,000 of the inhabitants, and seized as many more to be sold as slaves. He entered every court of the Temple, pillaged the treasury, and seized all the sacred utensils. He then commanded a great sow to be sacrificed on the altar of burnt offerings, part of the flesh to be boiled, and the liquor from the unclean animal to be sprinkled over every part of the Temple; and thus desecrated with the most odious defilement the sacred place which the Jews had considered for centuries the one holy spot in all the Universe.[2]

Two years afterwards, Antiochus determined to exterminate the Hebrew race from the face of the earth. This produced the revolt of the Jews under Mattathias, whose illustrious son, Judas Maccabæus, founded the Maccabæan dynasty. By 128 B.C., the Jews, under John Hyrcanus, recovered their complete independence, which they maintained until compelled to acknowledge the dominion of Rome.

But the native rulers could not govern for long without dissen-

---

2. Milman.

sion. Soon were two more competitors, Aristobulus and Hyrcanus, quarrelling about the succession to the Jewish throne. The republic of Rome, having trampled underfoot the pride and strength of the great Asiatic monarchies, assumed a right of interfering in the affairs of every independent kingdom. The ambassadors of Aristobulus and Hyrcanus appeared before Pompey, who was then in Syria and was at the zenith of his power. After subjugating Arabia, Pompey, in 63 B.C., marched directly into Judaea. Espousing the candidature of Hyrcanus, Pompey marched against Jerusalem, within the walls of which he was admitted by the party of Hyrcanus. Aristobulus and his supporters, with the priesthood, withdrew to the Temple and prepared for an obstinate defence.

At the end of three months, and after great loss of life, the Romans made themselves masters of the Temple.

> The conduct of the Roman general excited at once the horror and the admiration of the Jews. He entered the temple, and even penetrated and profaned with his heathen presence the Holy of Holies. All the riches he left untouched, and the temple he commanded to be purified from the carnage of his soldiers.[3]

He stipulated the tribute which the country was to pay, demolished the walls of the city, and nominated Hyrcanus to the priesthood, though without the royal diadem. The magnanimity of Pompey, in respecting the treasures of the temple, could not obliterate the deeper impression of Jewish hatred excited by his profanation of the sacred precincts.

From this time forward Judaea becomes more and more under the shadow of Rome. The walls of Jerusalem were rebuilt by Antipater, and later, the temple, which had become much dilapidated, was demolished, and rebuilt in great magnificence by Herod the Great. He was the last King of Judaea with any semblance of autonomy, and, in the year A.D. 6, Palestine was annexed to the Roman Empire.

We pass over the incidents in the life and death of our Lord, which, at the time, could have but little affected current events, but which were destined to influence so deeply the subsequent history, not merely of Palestine but of the whole world. And we come to the cataclysm of which Our Lord had been the sorrowful yet unerring Prophet.

Blinded by religious fanaticism, and convinced that God must fight

---

3. Milman.

upon their side and give victory to His chosen people, be their conduct never so cruel and their bearing never so arrogant, the Jewish race, though a mere handful of men, offered war to the mistress of the world. With little military organization or training, divided by factions and torn asunder by internal dissensions, they yet dared to defy the mighty power of Rome. They defeated the ill-starred expedition of Cestius Gallus, and inflicted upon the Roman arms the most terrible disgrace they had ever endured in the East. But the triumph was short-lived; a terrible revenge was at hand. It was in this year, *A.D.* 70, that Titus laid siege to the city.

At the time, its population was swollen ten or twenty-fold by the pilgrims attending the Passover. The reserves of food were destroyed in faction fights even before the Romans arrived outside the city walls.

> Of all wretched and bloody sieges in the world's history, few, if any, have been more wretched or more bloody than the siege of Jerusalem by Titus. Fierce and bloody as was the fighting, the deaths from sickness and famine were yet more terrible. Dead bodies were thrown out into the valleys, where they lay rotting, a loathsome mass. The number of those who died in the siege were estimated at 600,000. At night, miserable, starving wretches would steal into the ravines to gather roots for food; here they were pounced upon by ambushed Romans and crucified by hundreds next morning in full view of the battlements.[4]

Gradually the assaulting Romans got possession of portions of the city, yet the portions still uncaptured refused to surrender, their defenders still hoping against hope for a divine intervention, as in the days of Sennacherib. At length the city fell. The Romans, pouring in, began by slaying indiscriminately. Tiring of butchery, they turned their thoughts to plunder, but stood aghast at the houses filled with dead and putrefying corpses. The Temple of Herod was burnt, the city was desolate, while those whose miseries had not been relieved by death, were carried away into yet more miserable slavery or to a death more ignominious at Rome. As a Jewish city, Jerusalem had perished forever.

Sixty years later, Jerusalem was rebuilt by the Emperor Hadrian. He resolved to suppress altogether the troublesome and turbulent Judaism. The measures which he took caused the Jews to rise against him under Barcochebas. This was the wildest and the most bloodthirsty

---

4. Milman.

of all the Jewish revolts; but it was the last. Jerusalem having been recaptured, Hadrian converted it into a Roman colony, forbade Jews to approach, and built a temple of Jupiter on the site of the temple.

It was when the Roman Emperor Constantine embraced Christianity, and his mother Helena discovered the true Cross and the Holy Places, that Jerusalem came again into prominence. Thereafter, churches and monasteries sprung up throughout Palestine, which thus, for a time, became thoroughly Christianized, under the Christian emperors of Rome and Byzantium. But the seventh century saw the fall of the Christian ascendancy in Syria. In *A.D.* 614, the Persians, under Chosroes, swept through the land, massacring the Christians wholesale, and destroying most of their churches, including the Church of the Holy Sepulchre. The withdrawal of the Persians was followed by a brief return of Christian ascendancy lasting but eight years, under the Emperor Heraclius. And then, in 637, Jerusalem fell to the growing power of Islam. It was this new religion, with a calendar only dating from *A.D.* 622, which was to control the future destinies of the Holy City.

Islam arose at Mecca and Medina in barren and uninviting Arabia. When it started on that expansion, whereby it overspread half of the known world, Syria, from its situation, was naturally the first country to tempt its restless and devoted Arab warriors. Within ten years of the Hegira, or commencement of the Mahomedan era, we find the followers of the Prophet already in Syria. The Byzantine army was overwhelmed at the battle of the Yarmuk, and the Arabs laid siege to Jerusalem. The city capitulated to Omar, who granted terms of comparative magnanimity. His terms gave to the Christians security of person and property, safety of their churches, and non-interference on the part of Mahomedans with their religious exercises, houses or institutions.

Upon the site of the temple, which had been systematically defiled by the Christians out of abhorrence for the Jews, but which was honoured by the Moslems as the spot from which Mahomed ascended to heaven, was now erected the Mosque of Omar. This site became to the Mussulman, the most venerated spot in Jerusalem, as was the Church of the Holy Sepulchre to the Christian. When, in after years, pilgrimages to Mecca were temporarily interrupted, devout Mahomedans made the pilgrimage to Jerusalem instead.

For the next few centuries Christian and Muslim lived together upon a fairly workable basis of toleration. Massacres of Christians and destruction of their churches occurred periodically, either in revenge for Christian successes elsewhere, or in connexion with other Mussulman disorders when mutual assassination was popular. But, on the whole, pilgrims, who at this time swarmed from all over Europe to visit the Holy Places at Jerusalem, were allowed to do so comparatively unmolested—that is, they were probably not robbed more in Palestine than in other professedly Christian countries through which they had to pass along their road. Had the Arab Mussulman remained master of Jerusalem, the Christians of Europe would probably have remained content with the situation.

A change came in the year 1077. Jerusalem was then taken by the Turks, who had conquered all Asia Minor and were already threatening the Byzantine Empire in Europe. The treatment which the Christian pilgrims now received at Jerusalem aroused intense indignation in Europe, chiefly stimulated by the preaching of Peter the Hermit. Other motives there were, such as the protection of the Byzantine Empire from the menaces of the Turk, the desire of the Latin Church to prevail over the Byzantine, and the temptations always offered in a holy war of loot upon earth and salvation in heaven. Nevertheless, there undoubtedly spread, throughout Western Europe, a mighty wave of religious enthusiasm which was sincere.

The first Crusade was mainly recruited in France. Great were the vicissitudes through which the Crusaders passed on their pilgrimage through Europe and Asia Minor, largely through quarrels with their fellow-Christians before the Turks had even been encountered or their country entered. Having defeated the Turks at Antioch, the army marched south along the coast and at length reached and besieged Jerusalem. Of the numbers that set out from Western Europe, probably not less than a million, only a remnant of twenty thousand fighting men, with an equal number of followers, had reached the Holy City. Though thus decimated and war weary, the Crusaders were ecstatic with religious fervour; St. George was said to have appeared to them clad in shining armour; the Saracens gave way, and Jerusalem was taken by assault.

The usual massacre of the inhabitants followed, and estimates of the slain vary from forty to a hundred thousand. In 1099 was established the Christian kingdom of Jerusalem, the kingdom of the Crusaders, Latin in creed, French in nationality, feudal in character and precarious in existence. The state of affairs seems now rather to have resembled the relationship which formerly existed between the Hebrews and the Philistines, or, even more analogously, that between the Italian city-states of the Middle Ages. Most of the cities of Palestine were gradually annexed by the Christians, but some, notably Askalon, did not pass out of the hands of the Saracens for many decades. Accordingly, wars became matters of almost annual occurrence, and "never, during the whole eighty years of its existence, was the kingdom of Jerusalem free from war and war's alarms."[5]

The bulk of the original Crusaders left alive soon returned to their homes in Europe. There was little or no native Christian population on which to draw, and the kingdom became dependent for the support of its army, both as to men and money, on the pilgrims that swarmed from Europe to Jerusalem; naval assistance was given by Genoese and by Venetians, more, alas, from motives of commerce than of piety. Religious enthusiasm had been capable of conquering and establishing this kingdom, but it proved quite unequal to the tasks of sustenance or protection. And so, after eighty years of romance and trouble, of love and war, of lust and murder, often inflicted, more often endured, this kingdom fell, because it had no sure foundation.

The decline and fall of the Latin kingdom of Jerusalem forms a sordid story of jealousy, and intrigue, of futile ambition and divided counsels, of perjury and perfidy. The Crusaders intermarried with the women of the country, and, except so far as it was constantly recruited from Europe, the race rapidly degenerated. With no resources at their back, except the charity of Europe, the Crusaders yet had dreams of worldly aggrandisement, which included in their ken the whole of Egypt and Syria. The Second Crusade of 1146-9 came, not to conquer, but to support and defend this already tottering kingdom. It did that kingdom more harm than good, for it drained Europe of its potential pilgrims, anticipating and exhausting the natural flow of men and money on which the kingdom had come to rely, and dissipated them on a futile attempt to annex Damascus.

The Knights Templars,[6] the feudal barons of the country, built castles throughout the land, and lived at constant variance with the king and central government. Every baron fought for his own land and for his own aggrandisement. The kingdom of Jerusalem was fast tottering to its fall.

---

5. Besant & Palmer.

6. *The Military Religious Orders of the Middle Ages: The Knights Templar, Hospitaller and Others* by F. C. Woodhouse and *Knights of the Cross: Chronicle of the Fourth Crusade and The Conquest of Constantinople & Chronicle of the Crusade of St. Louis* by Geoffrey de Villehardin and Jean de Joinville are both also published by Leonaur.

It was in 1187 that Saladin, having made himself master of Egypt and of Damascus, attacked Tiberias, as a first step towards overthrowing the kingdom of Jerusalem. The Crusaders moved against him from Seffuriyeh. It was July, and the Crusaders were absolutely without water; the Saracens, with Lake Tiberias at their back, had abundance. The Crusaders, suffering terribly from thirst, nevertheless attacked. The result of the battle was a foregone conclusion. Here, at the Horns of Hattin, the Mount of Beatitudes, was the Crusaders' army destroyed and the power of the Christian completely crushed. Jerusalem itself, after a short, fierce struggle, fell in the following October. The inhabitants were not put to the sword. Huge ransoms were paid and the Christian population allowed to disperse throughout Syria. Jerusalem had passed again (it seemed as if forever) into the hands of the Mahomedan.

> The news of the fall of Jerusalem was received in Europe with a thrill of horror and indignation.[7]

Thereupon set forth the Third Crusade, that which is identified with Richard I of England. Travelling by sea, these Crusaders avoided the horrible sufferings inevitable to the crossing of Asia Minor. Acre was captured in 1190, by the Crusaders, after a siege lasting for two years. Thence they marched southwards, through Cæsarea to Jaffa, fighting on their way the great battle of Assur, when Saladin was defeated. But Richard, instead of marching upon Jerusalem, which lay in his grasp, vacillated and negotiated. At length he decided to go up against Jerusalem. Some twenty miles from the city he stopped. Again he vacillated. Dissensions broke out between the Duke of Burgundy and King Richard. The design of besieging Jerusalem was given up, and the army slowly and sadly returned to Jaffa. Thereupon, in 1192, a peace was concluded, whereby the sea coast, from Jaffa to Acre, was ceded to the Franks, but Jerusalem still remained in the hands of the Saracens.

There were several more Crusades. None of them (unless we except the treaty of the excommunicated Frederick in 1229) ever reached Jerusalem. Some of them never even reached Palestine, being shamefully diverted to other purposes. Saddest of all was the Children's Crusade, when fifty thousand poor misguided children followed the Cross (like the Pied Piper of Hamelin) to slavery, dishonour, or death. But these form no part of the history of Jerusalem.

---

7. Besant & Palmer.

In 1244, we find Christian and Saracen making common cause in Palestine against the Kharezmians. These Mongols, who only appeared on the stage of history for a brief period of four years, swept through the country, captured Jerusalem, massacred all on whom they could lay hands, Moslem and Christian alike, and destroyed such sacred relics as they could find. Then, defeated by the Egyptians, they perished out of history as suddenly as they had appeared.

In 1291, the Christians, by this time reduced to their last stronghold of Acre, were finally expelled by the Moslems from Palestine—and that was the end of the Crusades. Europe became reconciled to the fact that the Kingdom of Christ is a Kingdom, not of the sword but of the soul. And so, the watchword by which the Crusades were inspired now became the consolation of their end—"*Dieu le veut.*"

In 1400, Syria and Palestine fell under another Mongol invasion by Timoor the Tartar (Tamerlane). In 1517, Palestine was annexed to the Ottoman Empire under Selim I, of which Empire it has since formed an integral part. At the close of the eighteenth century, Napoleon marched through the country, defeating the Turks at Gaza and on the Plain of Esdraelon, but was forced to withdraw. In 1832, Mohammad Ali, having thrown off the Turkish yoke in Egypt, conquered Syria, but nine years later, through the action of the European Powers, the country was restored again to the Ottoman Porte.

In so far as any principles can be deduced from this history, they seem to show that Jerusalem, situated as it is, could never become the capital of a great Empire. On the other hand, this city, coveted by so many races and creeds, must be safeguarded by the arms and resources of some great Empire, or it can never remain at peace.

It may be of interest to close this *résumé* of the history of Jerusalem by comparing the route taken by General Allenby with those taken by previous soldiers in their conquests of Judaea. The routes taken by the British have already been fully described. In only one known case, that of the First Crusade, had Judaea been successfully invaded before by an invader who had not previously made himself master of at least three of her borders.[8] The attempt at a swift rush across one border made by Cestius Gallus, ended in a failure, which was only wiped out four years later after the Romans, under Vespasian and Titus, had first overrun Galilee and Samaria and mastered the strongholds round the Judaean borders. This was the policy followed, a thousand years later, by Saladin.

---

8. G. A. Smith

The upland of Judaea has almost never been invaded from the barren waterless south.[9] David, operating from Hebron, must have approached Jerusalem from the south, but he was already in possession of the Judaean plateau. The original attempt of the Israelites to enter the country from the south was checked, and they subsequently crossed the Jordan and entered Judaea through Jericho from the east. The Philistines must have come up by the passes from the west.

Sennacherib did not approach Jerusalem himself, but it was whilst warring against Egypt at Lachish (Tel el Hesi on the Maritime Plain) that he sent his arrogant message to Jerusalem; and it was on the plain that his victorious army, infected by the plague from Egypt, melted away as by a miracle. Egypt was his objective, not Judaea. Nebuchadnezzar may have invaded Judaea from the north, but it is more probable that he also came up from the west, after first making himself master of the Maritime Plain. Pompey was returning from his expedition in Arabia when he invaded, so he entered from the east, ascending the Judaean plateau by way of Jericho and Bethel. Herod invaded from the north.

In the Christian era, Cestius Gallus made his disastrous expedition by the Valley of Ajalon, Beth-horon and Gibeon. Titus, after the surrounding country had been subjugated, moved his army up to Jerusalem by Gophna (Jufna) and Bethel, and so through Bireh, from the north-west and north. The Moslems, in 637, first captured Damascus; subsequently they approached Jerusalem across the Jordan. The First Crusaders came through Asia Minor and won a decisive victory at Antioch; thence they came southward along the coast, through Ramleh, and up the Valley of Ajalon, their advance through the mountains being unopposed. Saladin, by the decisive battle of Hattin, near Tiberias, made himself master of the surrounding country before closing in upon Jerusalem, which he eventually did from Hebron (south), from Askalon (west), and from the north. In the Third Crusade, Richard and his Crusaders came oversea to Acre; after marching to Ramleh, they tried first to reach the Holy City up the Valley of Ajalon, and afterwards by the Vale of Elah, the Wady es Sunt, further to the south, but both attempts failed.

Many of the invading armies that have swept through Palestine have confined themselves to the great inter-continental road along the Maritime Plain, and have passed by Jerusalem, secure upon its plateau. We have seen that this was so with Sennacherib. This was probably

---

9. G. A. Smith.

the case with Alexander the Great, and was undoubtedly so with Napoleon. The latter defeated the Turks at Gaza and again on the Plain of Esdraelon. His objective was Syria, but he was foiled by the action of the British in the siege of Acre. This distraction also prevented him from making any attempt to reach Jerusalem.

Prior to the arrival of the British, it was seven centuries since a Christian conqueror had set foot in Jerusalem. But there was now no gloating of the Cross over the Crescent. On the contrary, guards of Moslem troops from our Indian Army were placed upon every building sacred to Islam, while Christian guards were mounted over those sacred to Christianity. Never before had Jerusalem fallen into the hands of conquerors so zealous for the safety of its populace or so concerned for the preservation of the city and all that it contained.

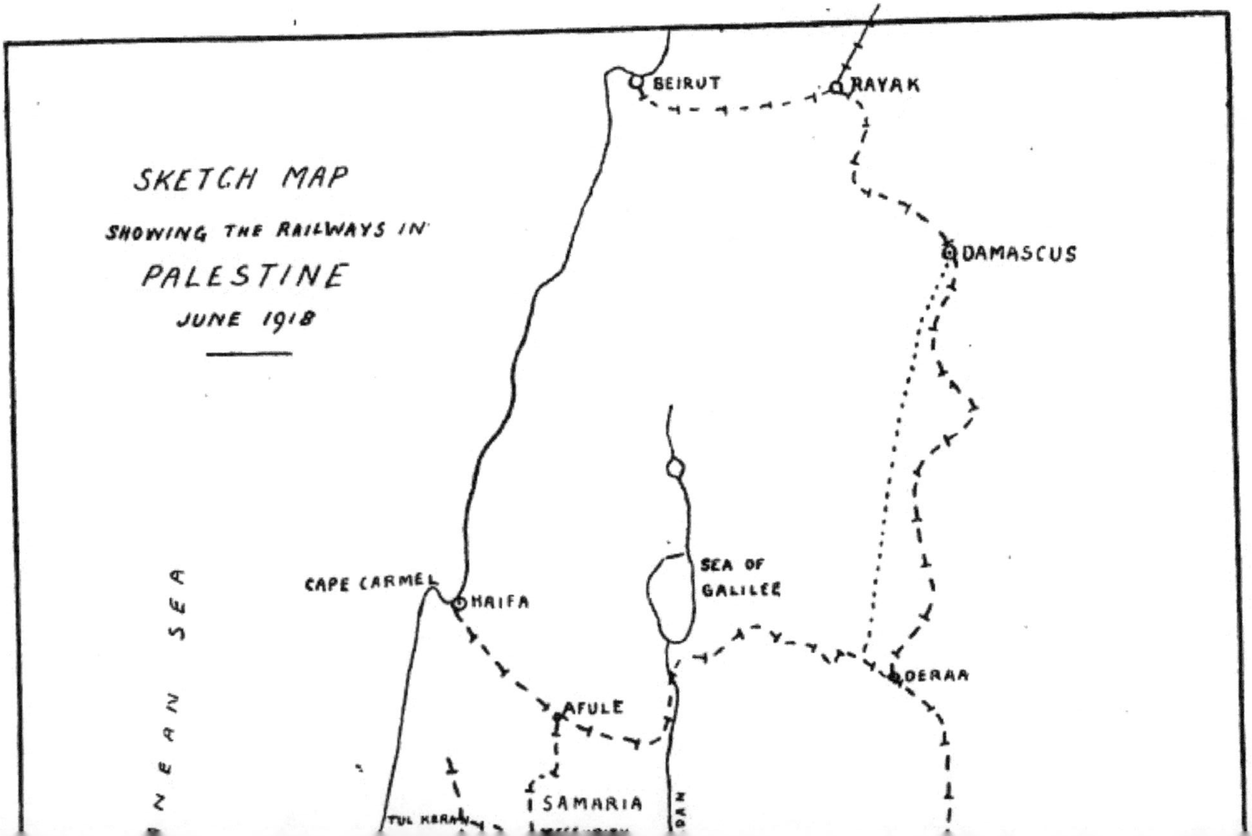

SKETCH MAP
SHOWING THE RAILWAYS IN
PALESTINE
JUNE 1918

DAMASCUS

RAYAK

BEIRUT

DERAA

SEA OF
GALILEE

AFULE

SAMARIA

HAIFA

CAPE CARMEL

TUL KERAM

MEDITERRANEAN SEA

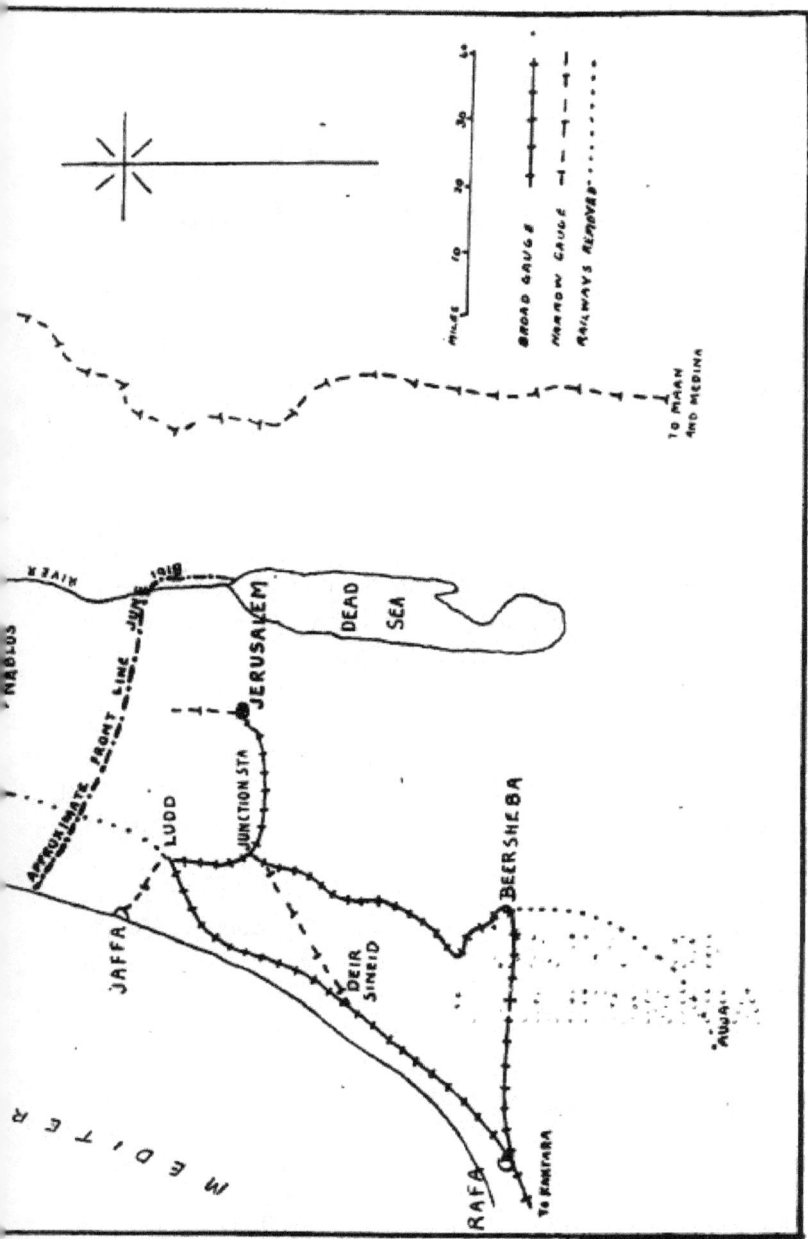

MEDITER

NABLUS

RIVER

JERUSALEM

DEAD SEA

APPROXIMATE FRONT LINE JUNE 1918

LUDD

JUNCTION STA

JAFFA

DEIR SINEID

BEERSHEBA

RAFA

TO KANTARA

AUJA

MILES

10 20 30 40

BROAD GAUGE
NARROW GAUGE
RAILWAYS REMOVED

TO MAAN AND MEDINA

CHAPTER 12

Junction Station and Ludd

An interesting task fell to my lot, in the reduction to order of the chaos existing at Junction Station. This place had been an important rest camp on the enemy's line of communications. That the Germans thought they had come to stay was manifested by the style in which the station and other buildings had been erected, as well as by the plans which they had left behind them for intended future development. Most of the buildings, including an up-to-date flour mill fitted with modern machinery, had been substantially built with stone. The erection of many additional houses was clearly contemplated, while the work had already been put in hand of planting fruit orchards.

The disgusting state in which these premises were left was indescribable. Rotting carcases of beasts lay all about the place, while other filth almost surpassed them in stench. The buildings were infested with flies by day and mosquitoes by night, while other forms of vermin carried on the good work throughout the whole twenty-four hours.

A large amount of stores had been left behind and had fallen into our hands, consisting mainly of grain, flour, and fodder (tibbin). The enemy had destroyed some of the buildings, smashed up the mill machinery, and set on fire as much of the corn as possible. This fire lasted for days, until at length it burned itself out, for it was useless attempting to salve any portion of the grain composing the bonfire.

Before we had so much as taken possession, swarms of Bedouin came through the premises to loot. Thieving with them is instinctive. They could not understand why they had not a right to help themselves to what the Turks had abandoned. However, a strong guard was posted at once; those Bedouin who had taken up their abode on the premises were evicted; and preparations were made to face a somewhat stormy night.

All that night through the crack of rifles resounded. Although the bag next morning proved to be small, yet, for days afterwards, Bedouin kept dropping in at our hospitals with bullet wounds to be dressed, as to the cause of which they could offer no satisfactory explanation. After this the looting fell off considerably. Nevertheless, a certain number of looters, averaging about a dozen a day, were caught and put into the guardroom. We were glad of their assistance, as there was much filthy cleaning up to be done, so, fools that came to loot, remained to scavenge. Once we had an awkward predicament, for the sergeant of the guard, having confined in the same lock-up some looters, whose detention should be for twenty-four hours, and some prisoners, whose detention should be for the duration of the war, could not subsequently tell them apart.

The enemy left here intact an entire Turkish hospital. It was one of the most picturesque of Eastern sights that anybody could wish to see. Crowded together in one huge ward were men of every shade, in variegated costumes, lying on beds with coverlets rivalling Joseph's coat of many colours. Unfortunately, the hospital was infected, or suspected of infection, with typhus. Therefore, as soon as the patients and staff had been evacuated, it was set on fire, and the whole hospital, woodwork, tents and all that they contained, ascended to heaven in a great column of smoke. Among the contents was a nice new camp bedstead. Pending the decision as to the competent military authority in whose custody this should be placed, I gave orders for it to be transferred to my quarters.

But, strangely enough, each senior officer that arrived considered that the competent military authority to take charge of this bedstead was himself. It must have had at least a dozen owners by the time that it ascended in smoke. This hospital also contained one case of sardines. It was wonderful how widely spread became the fame of those sardines. Every British officer in Palestine seems to have licked his lips and looked forward to a meal of sardines when he should pass through Junction Station. Unfortunately, nobody could find those sardines. But a week later, when the rush of officers had gone, it was discovered that they had been appropriated as medical comforts by the R.A.M.C. Now, it so happened, that none of the patients then arriving were on a sardine diet, so other measures had to be taken to ensure that the sardines were not wasted.

As the army went forward, they sent back large numbers of Turkish prisoners of war. These were collected at Junction Station, where a compound was formed. Such as were required for labour were temporarily detained, while the others were marched back under guard to railhead.

During this sojourn, the prisoners were usefully employed in clearing up the messes which had been left behind, particularly in burying carcases. At one place we found half-a-dozen dead buffaloes lying half submerged. Before they could be got at and cleared away it was necessary to drain off the water. A party of the prisoners were detailed for this task; a few hours later they were found seriously trying to drain this water away up-hill. Among the prisoners were a few officers. In default of other suitable accommodation, one of them was allowed to live in a room at the Commandant's house. He displayed great anxiety lest somebody should touch the disused telephone or other wires, fire a booby trap possibly left behind by his kind friends, and so blow him to eternity.

There was not much time to spare for contemplation. Nevertheless, in this, the Vale of Sorek, I often thought of Samson and Delilah, and "*Mon cœur s'ouvre à ton voix*"; or, pictured the ark of the covenant wend its way past my very door, on a cart drawn by two milch kine, on that wonderful journey from Ekron to Beth-Shemesh.

There was plenty of work to be done, in reducing chaos to order, in protecting much valuable property, in meeting the requirements of thousands of passing troops, and in spreading, as it were, the spawn for this mushroom town. It had been an important place under Turkish administration. It promised, under the British *régime*, to become the most important railway centre in Palestine. Consequently, schemes of water supply, sanitation, and town planning had to be evolved and installed immediately, hospitals opened in the most appropriate buildings, spaces set apart for camping grounds for all classes of troops and animals, huge dumps and supply dumps respectively, railway sidings laid down and cemeteries opened both for Christians and for Mahomedans, while roads had to be improved and sign-boards set up in all directions.

Many and diverse were the arrivals and departures in the course of one busy week. Foremost came the fighting troops of the 21st Corps, the 75th and 54th Divisions, followed later by those of the 20th Corps, the 60th and 74th Divisions. With them arrived field ambulances, which took possession of the best of the buildings and converted them into hospitals. Companies of Royal Engineers arrived, and travelling workshops staffs of the Ordnance Department, and both of these lost no time in opening their workshops. Enormous supply dumps were formed and camel convoys, miles long, arrived with supplies. The camels were specially inconsiderate, and would select awkward spots, like cross-roads, at which to lie down and die. They were welcome to die, if only they could and would have first made adequate arrangements for their own obsequies. A battalion of British West Indians that arrived, aroused both sympathy and amusement. They had marched through torrential rain and arrived soaked to the skin. In spite of a warning as to what they might expect, they rushed for shelter into some of the buildings which had not yet been disinfected; but their exit was even faster than their entrance, and they preferred the wet and cheerless exterior to being eaten alive within.

Scarcely a day's march behind the fighting troops, arrived a thousand or more of the Egyptian Labour Corps. These were immediately set to work on the roads, and such good work did they do that the roads were soon in an excellent condition for mechanical transport. Full of irony was the arrival of several guards and a staff of military police *en route* for Jerusalem. It was believed, at this time, that the fall of Jerusalem was imminent. That Britain's fair name might not be sullied by any foolish misbehaviour, or any still more foolish collection of souvenirs, it was decided that guards should at once be mounted upon the Holy Places in Jerusalem.

These guards, Christian and Moslem, collected at Junction Station, ready to march straight into the city; but, when its fall was postponed *sine die*, they had sadly but surely to return to their own regiments. The intention had been to surround Jerusalem with a cordon of British sentries; an order, accordingly, was published that any British soldier found within 5 miles of Jerusalem would be liable to be shot. Our unfortunate British soldiers fighting on Neby Samwil, which was within the prescribed distance, readily endorsed that sentiment, though scarcely in the sense implied by the authorities.

Of all activities at this time of industry, none were greater than those of the railway development companies of the Royal Engineers. The Turkish line had been destroyed in several places and the rolling stock much damaged. Nevertheless, repairs were put in hand immediately, leaky engines were made water-tight, damaged trucks and coaches were made fit to travel, and, within a very short space of time, there was a train running each way between Junction Station and Deir Sineid. As being the services of primary importance, the first trains were confined to the bringing up of ammunition and the taking down of wounded. The captured rolling stock was limited, and so the number of trains was painfully restricted.

Fortunately, this narrow gauge line was of similar gauge to certain light railways in Egypt, and rolling stock from those lines was brought up with all convenient speed. Moreover, two quite new engines, said to have been originally destined for this line but captured at sea during the early days of the war, were hurried up and put into commission. New constructional work was also put in hand at once, including an embankment for continuing the line northwards across the bed of the Wadi Surar (Sorek), the original steel girder bridge having unfortunately been destroyed. The fate of the bridges here was similarly unfortunate. The railway bridge, which should have been blown up before, so as to prevent the escape of the Turkish trains, was only destroyed after they had got away; and so the destruction of this bridge proved of great hindrance to us, but caused no inconvenience whatever to the enemy.

The other bridge across the *wadi* was a timber bridge, which carried the road. As this bridge was insecure and required strengthening, a party of military police were posted upon it to stop all traffic from crossing it through the night. Seized with a brain wave, they lit a fire upon the centre of the bridge. This expedient proved so successful, that it not only stopped the traffic for that night, but for all time. When morning came, it was discovered that they had burnt away the bridge itself, and a new bridge had to be constructed.

An armoured train was improvised from such trucks as were available, the sides being sandbagged and a Lewis gun mounted in front. With this, the railway line was patrolled towards Jerusalem for some miles, until destroyed bridges made further progress impossible. The result of this reconnaissance showed that trains could run for some distance along this line, and ammunition trains were pushed forward accordingly.

When I left Junction Station to rejoin the fighting troops, it was well on the high road to importance and fame. This, however, never matured. It was to the policy of railway construction that this place owed its primary existence; it was to an extension of that policy that it looked for its future development; it was through a change in that policy that its glory soon afterwards departed.

The original intention had been to adapt to our use the Turkish railway system, merely broadening the gauge. In that case, our own broad gauge line from Kantara, which, immediately on the fall of Gaza, had been brought through to Deir Sineid, would have been continued along the route of the Turkish line from Deir Sineid to Junction Station. The first months of working this Turkish line, still in its narrow gauge condition as captured, did not afford a promising outlook. These were months of torrential and persistent rain. The country became a quagmire. Landslips along the permanent way, and the washing away of culverts, became of such frequent occurrence, that it was decided to abandon this portion of this line altogether.

Committed, therefore, to no predetermined route, the engineers were left with the whole country open to them to choose a course for their new trunk railway to the north. They chose a line much nearer the coast, and approximately followed the border line between the fertile plain and the sand dunes from Deir Sineid as far north as Yebna, thence bearing north-east towards Ramleh and Ludd. This had the effect of making the future railhead at Ludd.

Situate at the cross-roads where the Valley of Ajalon debouches upon the plain, and the ancient route from Jerusalem to Jaffa crosses the yet more ancient route from Egypt and Gaza to Acre and Damascus, the neighbourhood of Ramleh and Ludd has for many centuries been the site of an important town. In Biblical days it was Ludd; in Crusading days it was Ramleh. The towns are but a couple of miles apart. And so it came about that now, once again, this spot became the great traffic junction of Palestine.

As time passed on, and as, through the spring and summer of 1918, we held a line across Palestine to the north of and covering Jerusalem and Jaffa, railway development proceeded apace, being focussed on Ludd. In spite of the difficulties of railway engineering in the mountains, the broad gauge line was carried from Ludd through Junction Station right up to Jerusalem. Well-constructed narrow gauge lines were laid down between Ludd and Jaffa, and between railhead and various distributing centres close behind the front line. The line from Junction Station to Beersheba was changed from narrow to broad gauge and extended to Rafa.

Thereafter the line was double from Kantara to Rafa. From Rafa, one single line went forward, by Belah, Gaza and Yebna, to Ludd, while another single line went forward to Ludd by way of Beersheba and Junction Station. The advantages of a double line system north of Rafa were thus secured at times of pressure by working the full freight trains forward to Ludd *viâ* Gaza and Yebna, and working the trains of returned empties back again by way of Beersheba.

Ludd developed apace. Soon were seen all the evidences and activities of a great advanced base and distributing centre. Huge ordnance and supply dumps arose, workshops and depots were to be seen on all sides, a great bakery was installed and even a mineral-water factory. The importance of Ludd far eclipsed the quondam glory of Belah, and came nearer to rivalling that of Kantara.

To an Englishman, the chief interest of Ludd lies in its being the place of martyrdom and burial of St. George. Was it not appropriate that the victorious British armies in Palestine should have been provided and fed from beside the very tomb of their own Patron Saint?

CHAPTER 13

The Jordan

Jerusalem having surrendered on the 9th December, the enemy lay round about in an encircling line on the north and east. The first thing to be done was to make good our hold upon the city. Accordingly, a series of minor operations took place, with the object of clearing the enemy from any points of vantage that he held and driving him further from the city.

On the night of the 26/27th December, determined counter-attacks were delivered by the Turks. They attacked the 53rd Division at points east of Jerusalem, and the 60th to the north, their principal objective being Tel el Ful, a conspicuous hill 3 miles east of Neby Samwil, from which Jerusalem and the intervening ground could be overlooked. On the morning of the 28th, a lull occurred in the fighting, followed by an attack of unexpected strength against the whole front. The successes gained by this attack were short-lived. A counter-attack by the 74th and 10th Divisions, further to the left, now made itself felt. This was launched against the enemy's reserves, and thus deprived the enemy of the initiative.

The Turkish attack being spent, a general advance northward, took place, not, however, without further heavy fighting. Pursuing our advantage, we further advanced our line on the 30th, and occupied a line from Beitior (Bethel), 2 miles north-east of Bireh, to Janieh and Ras Kerker, 7 miles west, north-west of Bireh. Bireh, which had been our objective in November, was, at last, securely in our possession. The Turkish attempt to recapture Jerusalem had ended in crushing defeat.

Throughout the winter months the weather was miserably wet, and the troops in Palestine, whether engaged in active operations or merely holding the line, suffered intense discomfort. The mails brought us letters from our friends at home, saying how much they envied us who were spending Christmas in the Holy Land. But those who were up the line spent Christmas Day soaked to the skin in a gale of wind and rain, while their Christmas dinner consisted of half-rations of bully beef and biscuit. They were wishing themselves anywhere else upon this earth. The appalling weather conditions made it impossible to get more than the bare necessities of life forward from railhead, and tons of Christmas luxuries sent from England through Egypt lay soaked and rotting in dumps at Deir Sineid.

January was much too wet for operations in this country. In February, however, General Allenby determined on the capture of Jericho. The country from round Jerusalem slopes down, as we have seen, very abruptly to Jericho and the Jordan Valley. Precipitous slopes, rocky ridges and narrow ledges, confined the advance to definite lines on which the enemy could concentrate fire. The advance began on the 19th, and, by the evening of the 20th, the 60th Division had reached a line 4 miles west of the cliffs overlooking Jericho.

In the meantime, the mounted troops were working on the right or south of the infantry, towards the commanding position of Neby Musa, near the north-west corner of the Dead Sea. This advance was held up at the last *wadi* which was directly overlooked by, and subjected to, a heavy fire from Neby Musa. Other mounted troops, further to the right, discovered a way down to the Jordan Plain, where they were firmly established by dusk. That night the Turks withdrew, and our mounted troops, moving up the Plain, entered Jericho on the morning of the 21st.

There are two or three routes between Jericho and the summit of the Judaean plateau. That by which the British had now come down was not the route followed by Joshua and the Israelites. They, on the other hand, ascended by a route farther north, through Mukhmas (Michmash) and Beitin (Bethel), thus reaching the summit near Bireh. The route followed by the pilgrims was that of the main road, which hereafter became the main line of supply of the forces operating in this direction.

Having secured Jericho and the low country beyond as far as the Jordan, operations were now commenced with the object of pushing the enemy northwards, and clearing him from another substantial portion of Palestine. This would, at the same time, broaden the base for future operations which were contemplated across the River Jordan.

Operations on a large scale were commenced on March 9th. Both the 20th and 21st Corps were engaged. We will, however, consider here only the operations of the 20th Corps, leaving those of the 21st until a subsequent chapter. The reader is already familiar with the type of country, which resembled that between Jerusalem and Jericho. The downward slopes were exceptionally steep, in places precipitous. The slopes were swept by machine-gun and rifle fire, and the beds of the *wadis* were enfiladed. The ascent on the far side was steeply terraced. Men had alternately to hoist and pull each other up under fire, and finally to expel the enemy from the summits in hand-to-hand fighting. Under these conditions no rapid advance could be looked for.

The 60th Division, by night, crossed the Wadi el Auja, north of Jericho (not to be confused with the *wadi* of the same name to the north of Jaffa). This division seized a position astride the Beisan-Jericho road. The 53rd Division captured Tel-Asur, a conspicuous landmark among a mass of high hills, which mountain the enemy tried repeatedly, but in vain, to recover. Farther to the left, a counter-attack was repulsed by the 10th Division. At the conclusion of the operations, the high ground covering the approaches to the Jordan by the Jericho-Beisan Road had been secured, and also, farther west, linking up with the 21st Corps, the high ground stretching across the hills of Mount Ephraim.

We come now to the passage of the River Jordan and the operations in Eastern Palestine. It will be remembered, from what has already been written,[1] that active operations were in progress about this time between the Turks south-east of the Dead Sea and our Arab allies, the troops of the King of the Hejaz. The Turkish line of communications ran down the Hejaz Railway through eastern Palestine, temptingly near our forces at Jericho. It will also be remembered,[2] that the Jordan Valley, and ascent therefrom into the hills of Eastern Palestine are unique. It would therefore have been difficult or impossible to cut the Turks' Hejaz communications by maintaining a permanent garrison astride the railway, such garrison being based on Jericho with an extremely vulnerable line of communications across the valley. It was thought, however, that much useful service might be rendered to the Arabs if a raiding force were to cross the Jordan and destroy the railway in the neighbourhood of Amman.

The country between the Jordan and Amman offered many obstacles to our advance. There were the marshes of the Jordan Valley to be crossed, ridges of clay to be surmounted, scrub to be negotiated,

---

1. See before chapter 3.
2. See before chapter 4.

followed by an ascent of 3,500 feet. The metalled road to Amman crosses the Jordan at the Ghoraniyeh Bridge, and reaches the hills at Shunet Nimrin. It then winds up a *wadi* to Es Salt, whence it strikes due eastward to Amman.

The operations commenced in the latter part of March. No serious obstacle was encountered until the crossings of the Jordan were reached. A small party was sent in motor-boats across the Dead Sea to dispose of any enemy who might be in the district to the north-east of the Dead Sea, but they met with few traces of the enemy. The enemy had destroyed the bridge at Ghoraniyeh early in the month. Other means had therefore to be devised for effecting a crossing. "*Jordan over-floweth all his banks all the time of harvest.*" On the 28th March, owing to heavy rain, the river rose 9 feet. Floods had, therefore, to be contended with. The current is at all times rapid, and the banks, on account of the floods, are boggy and difficult for the approach of transport.

On the night of the 21st/22nd March, the main crossings of the river were attempted, both at Ghoraniyeh, and a few miles further south at Hajlah, where the Pilgrim Road from Jerusalem reaches the Jordan. At the former point three attempts to swim the river were made, under fire, by men with ropes attached to their bodies, but in each case the swimmers were carried away by the strong current and found it impossible to reach the opposite bank. Then a punt was launched, but this was no sooner launched than it was swept away. The attempt was commenced in the bright moonlight, but was much hampered by enemy fire. It was renewed after the moon had gone down, but then it was impossible to find the easiest route or to negotiate the current in the dark.

Farther downstream, however, the efforts met with better fortune. A small party succeeded in swimming across in the dark and landing on the left bank. These towed a rope behind them, by which, after landing, they hauled across light rafts. The crossing by the raft-loads of men had to be carried out in the face of some hostile fire. Portions of the scrub had been set on fire by the enemy, and these fires to some extent lit up the rafts as they were being pulled across. By daylight, 300 men had been got across, and a small bridge-head established. A barrel bridge was without delay constructed by the engineers. Very little progress could be made that day as the scrub was infested with enemy machine guns. On the following night, however, a rush was made, and the bridge-head enlarged to a width of 1,500 yards. That night the engineers constructed a steel pontoon bridge, and an entire cavalry regiment was passed over by dawn. The cavalry soon cleared away the enemy, not only from Hajlah, but also from in front of Ghoraniyeh. Bridges were built now at Ghoraniyeh and the passage of the river assured.

Having successfully crossed the Jordan, the force pushed on eastwards across the low country, meeting with some opposition. Eventually we reached Shunat Nimrin. The enemy retreating up the Es Salt road were bombed and machine-gunned by our aircraft. Part of our force, following on their heels, entered Es Salt on the 25th, while, on the 26th, our mounted troops occupied Amman. The railway to the south of the station was successfully cut, but north of Amman the cutting was not complete. Consequently, the enemy were able to receive considerable reinforcements. Before Amman could be attacked in strength some 4,000 Turks were in position covering the viaduct and tunnel, while 2,000 more were moving on Es Salt from the north. Five miles of railway line were however, destroyed, while much other damage was done to the railway line. But, in view of the strength of the enemy and the difficulties of our communications (we had only been able to bring forward mountain-artillery), our force withdrew.

The raid had not entirely fulfilled its object, but much good work had been done, and it had materially assisted Sherif Faisal with his Hejaz troops in his operations further south against Maan.

Our force returning from Eastern Palestine did not abandon the hardly-won eastern bank of the Jordan. Bridge-heads were retained. The Turks, however, became aggressive, and, on the 11th April, attacked our bridge-head at Ghoraniyeh. They were repulsed from here and driven back to Shunet Nimrin, which they strongly garrisoned.

On the 30th April another raid was made across the Jordan. This time our infantry attacked the Shunet Nimrin position, while the cavalry, intending to cut off the garrison, moved round the flank and reached Es Salt. But a strong Turkish force, crossing the Jordan from the Nablus area at Jisr ed Damieh, drove back the cavalry, who lost nine guns in their retirement. This raid had been planned to co-operate with the Beni Sakr Arabs. Their promised assistance did not materialize, and the whole force was brought back to the crossings of the Jordan.

Thenceforth, until the sweep of the following September the Jordan river and bridge-heads remained our front line.

CHAPTER 14

The Wadi Deir Ballut

In the last chapter we saw how, after the capture of Jerusalem, the 20th Corps proceeded to improve the line on the right. We will now follow the operations of the 21st Corps on the left.

The first operation of importance was that carried out by the 52nd Division on the extreme left. On the night of the 20th/21st December, 1917, crossings, partly by fording and partly by rafts, were effected over the Wadi Auja, a few miles to the north of Jaffa. The high ground overlooking the *wadi* from the north was rushed before dawn, and a line was consolidated which effectually deprived the enemy of all observation from the north over the Valley of the Wadi Auja. Incidentally, the distance between the enemy and Jaffa was increased from 3 to 8 miles. This safeguarded Jaffa and its harbour, and the main Jaffa-Jerusalem road. Further adjustments of the line were made, including the capture of Rantieh on the railway and El Tine and Bornat to the right, which gave commanding views over the forward country and increased elbow room to the troops covering Ludd and Ramleh.

As the result of these operations the line ran, at the beginning of March, approximately as follows. The 60th Division on the right had reached the Jordan, our line running along that river as far north as the Wadi Auja and then bending westwards. On their left came the 53rd Division, a little to the north of Bireh, and on their left again the 10th Division completed the front of the 20th Corps. They joined up the 75th Division, whose frontage ran from Midieh (the Modin of the Maccabees) through Kibbiah to the foot-hills at Et Tireh; from here the 54th Division extended across the plain; while the 52nd Division held the sector close to the sea, a little to the north of the other Wadi Auja.

Except for occasional rains, our soldiering in the 75th Division sector, throughout February and the early part of March, was campaigning *de luxe*. The enemy had gone right back to the line of the Wadi Deir Ballut, leaving a No Man's Land in front of us about 4 miles across. He held advanced posts a mile or two in front of our line, but his guns had been taken well back out of range. We therefore enjoyed immunity both from sniping and shelling, and could move about in front of our line without anxiety, even in broad daylight. The observation posts that we occupied commanded extensive views across No Man's Land, and we should have had early intimation had there been any considerable hostile movement.

We thus had opportunities for training, and preparing ourselves for the next forward push. The whole battalion was put through a course of musketry. The forward slopes of our position provided an admirable field firing range, with all No Man's Land for the stray bullets to spend themselves upon. How it must have made the Turk itch to see men lying about in platoons in the open before his very eyes, and how he must have longed to have had a gun within range, and to have dispersed us with a few rounds of shrapnel. We also instituted a very successful shooting-gallery. In the front line beer was seldom procurable, though much appreciated. Such as we were able to obtain from the canteen was taken to the rifle range. An empty bottle was set up 200 yards in front of the firer and a full one behind him. If he hit the former he became entitled to the contents of the latter. Each man was entitled to one free shot, and as many more as he liked at a cost of a penny each. The result was, that, at a very nominal cost to the canteen funds, the individual shooting of the battalion considerably improved.

Aerial activity was interesting. We soon became accustomed to the distinctive hum of the Hun machines flying high above us, followed by the barking of our "Archies." Then we could trace the track of the planes across the sky by the line of white smoke puffs left by our bursting archy shells. Archy seldom reckons to get a direct hit on a plane, but, by the expenditure of quantities of ammunition, he makes the Hun fly too high to see anything of value or to drop bombs with much hope of success. More tangible results were obtained by our fighting planes, which engaged the Hun in the air. A pretty little fight took place a thousand feet or so above our heads, between two of our planes and a couple of Huns. After preliminary circling and manoeuvring for place, during which one Hun machine discreetly went all out for home, one of our planes swooped straight on to the remaining

SKETCH MAP

OF COUNTRY ROUND

RAFA.T

ILLUSTRATING OPERATIONS, MARCH TO
SEPTEMBER 1918.

APPROXIMATE BRITISH LINE AT
COMPLETION OF SPRING OFFENSIVE —+++++++

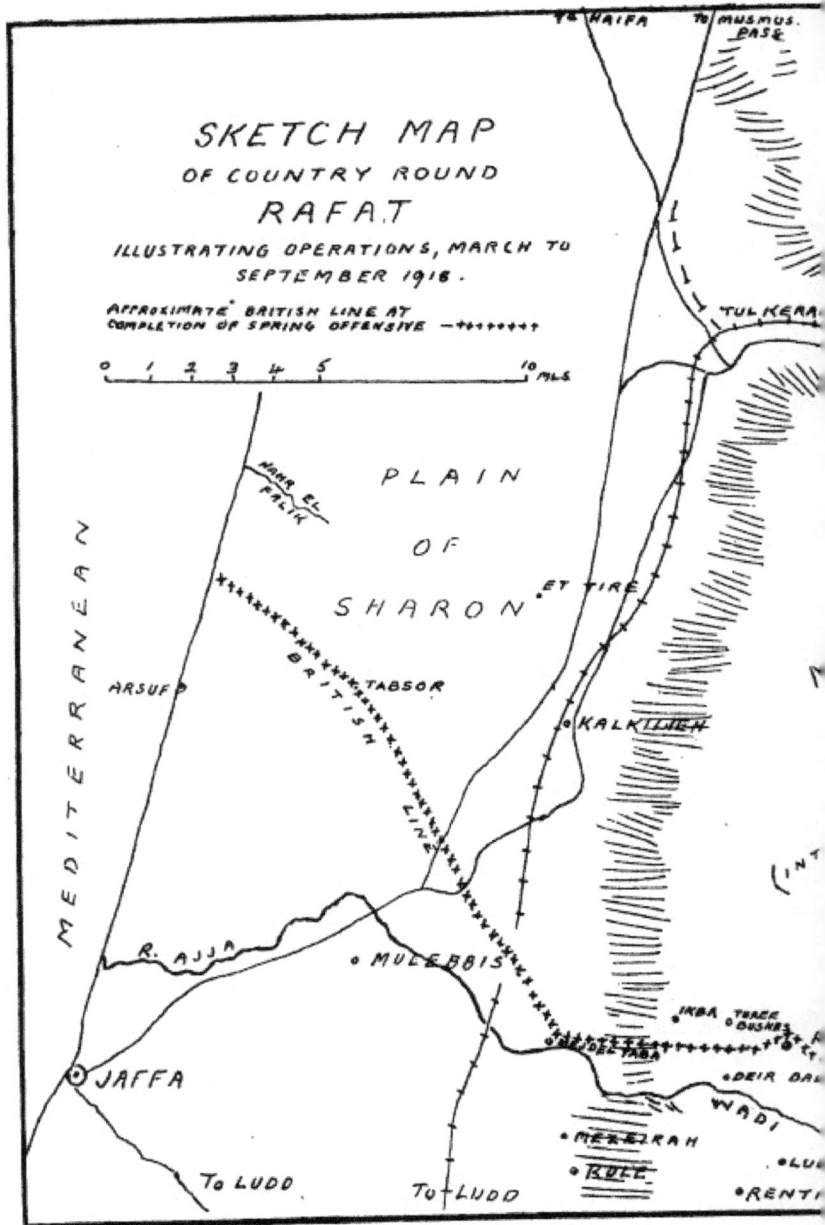

0 1 2 3 4 5 10 MLS.

TO HAIFA   TO MUSMUS.
                    PASS

TUL KERA

PLAIN

OF

SHARON

ET TIRE

MEDITERRANEAN

NAHR EL
FALIK

BRITISH LINE

TABSOR

ARSUF

KALKILIEH

R. AJJA

MULEBBIS

JAFFA

IKBA THREE
      BUSHES

MEJDEL YABA

DEIR BAL

MEZEIRAH

WADI

KULE

TO LUDD   TO LUDD

RENTI

LUB

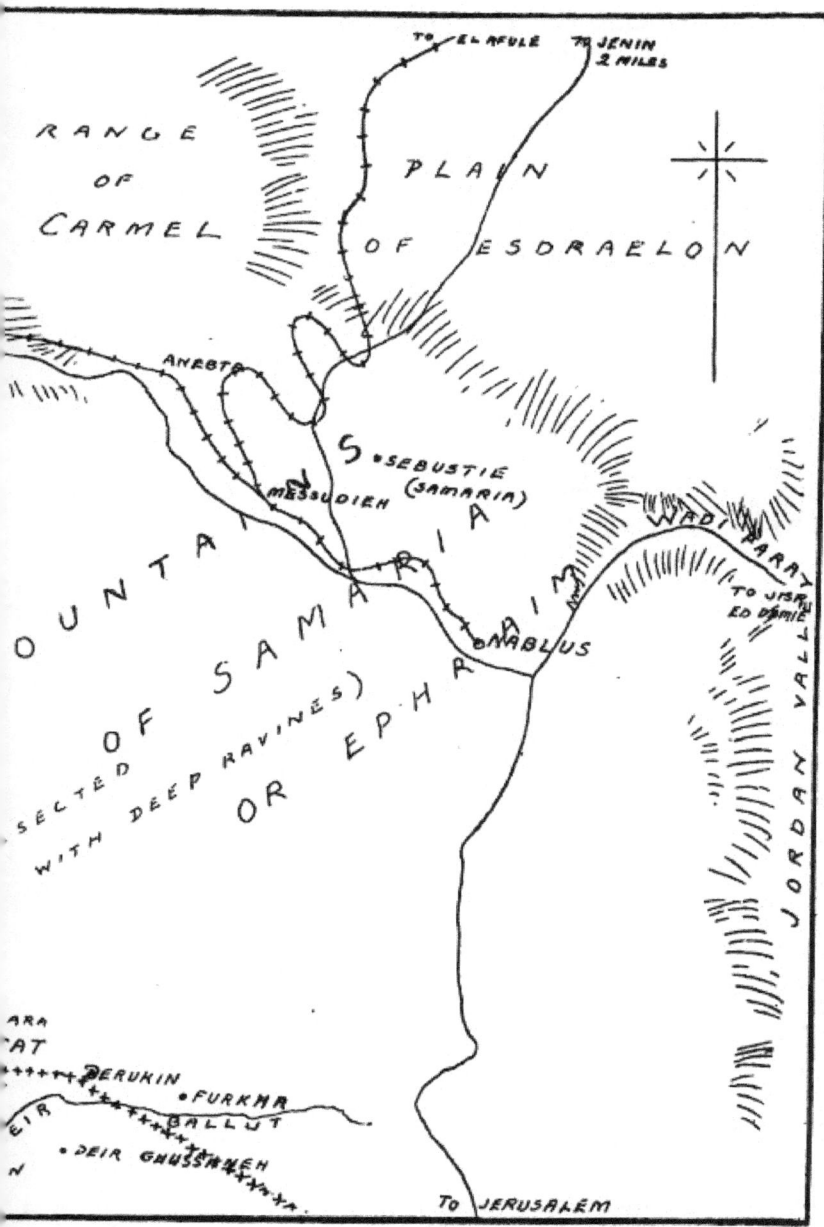

RANGE
OF
CARMEL

PLAIN

OF ESDRAELON

TO EL AFULE   TO JENIN
2 MILES

ANEBTA

S
•SEBUSTIE
(SAMARIA)

MESSUDIEH

OUNTA   I A
OF SAMARIA
SECTED   WADI FARAH
WITH DEEP RAVINES)   OR EPHRAIM
•NABLUS   TO JISR
                           ED DAMIE

JORDAN VALL

ARA
AT
+ + + + • BERUKIN • FURKHA
EIR   BALLUT
N   • DEIR GHUSSANEH

TO JERUSALEM

Hun, pouring a burst of Lewis gun fire into the pilot and observer at short range.

Badly wounded, the Hun pilot turned his machine full speed for home. But our other plane, which had retained its altitude, hovered over him, headed him off from home, and shepherded him down on to the plain, where he was forced to land and was captured. On another occasion, we were puzzled to see a Hun plane, returning from our lines, pitch in enemy territory, and, though unattacked, go up in smoke and flame. Subsequent reports furnished an explanation. The Hun pilot had descended without being very sure of his whereabouts. The Turks, mistaking him for a Britisher, opened fire upon him with a machine gun. Thereupon, believing himself to be in hostile territory, the pilot burnt his machine and surrendered—to his own friends!

Campaigning *de luxe*! The wild flowers did all that lay in their power to add to the luxury. The warm sun of February and March, following the drenching rain of the winter, produces in Palestine a profusion of beautiful flowers that is probably surpassed nowhere. The countryside was literally carpeted with choice flowers of sweet smell and varied colour. To mention but a few—there were red, white, and blue anemones; cyclamen, white, pink and mauve; aromatic herbs; poppies and corn-flowers; scarlet tulips; pink phlox; blue irises, velvety arum lilies, black and crimson, tall, stately hollyhocks. And the catalogue is scarce begun. Truly a floral Paradise!

Early in March came rumours of a forward move. The nominal pretext was an improvement of our line. Other motives may possibly have been influencing the higher authorities, such as keeping the initiative in our hands, fostering an aggressive spirit, and feeling the strength of the enemy with a view to subsequent operations on a larger scale.

Almost opposite Jaffa the central range of Judaean hills is cleft by a great gorge. Starting at a point on the edge of, and almost overlooking the Jordan Valley, it runs approximately due east and west, with many turns and even hairpin bends, until it debouches on the plain at Mejdel Yaba, thence forming a main tributary of the River Auja. In the days of the Maccabees this gorge formed the frontier between the Jews and the Samaritans. This gorge is the Wadi Deir Ballut. The sides of this *wadi* are at all points steep, at some precipitous, presenting in places an almost sheer drop of several hundred feet. The bed of the *wadi* is from a hundred to a couple of hundred yards wide and the surface level. Thus the Wadi Ballut formed an admirable defensive line for the Turk; after it had passed into our hands, it provided us with an admirable line of communication.

The Turk, at this time, held the line of the Wadi Ballut with such advanced posts as could deny to our patrols all access to the *wadi*. Available information about the *wadi* was thus restricted to reports and maps, and was none too ample or reliable. The intermediate country consisted of approximately flat "*merjs*," intersected with *wadis*, and dotted about with hills, villages, and other features of tactical importance. At this time of the year it somewhat resembled the general appearance of Exmoor. For several days prior to the advance patrols were sent out into No Man's Land, that as much as possible might be ascertained about, and as many as possible be made familiar with, the terrain over which we had to operate.

On the 12th March, the whole 75th Division, in co-operation with the divisions on its flanks, moved forward. The operations of this day were perhaps little more than minor operations, certainly not one of the decisive battles of the war, although their effect in drawing reinforcements to Palestine may have had far-reaching results in other zones such as Mesopotamia. Nevertheless, as they formed such a pretty field day, so like our manoeuvres at home, I venture upon a short description, in the hope that it may be of interest to those whose soldiering experience has been confined to the home front. There was no horrid barbed wire to contend with, nor gas. There were not even trenches, for the Turks' defence work here consisted only of stone walls, technically known as *sangars*. During the commencing stages we were not even shelled.

Shortly after dawn, our heavy artillery opened the ball by shelling the advanced posts of the enemy. At seven o'clock the whole line moved forward. Our first objective, a prominent knoll, was 4,000 yards away, and no previous opposition was expected. Having assumed the appropriate formation before crossing the crest, we moved forward in "artillery" formation, that is to say, in lines of platoons in file. For the non-military reader, it should be explained that this is the formation in which troops are considered least vulnerable against artillery or distant rifle and machine-gun fire. Great care was taken to ensure that direction was maintained, an officer with compass being specially detailed for this purpose, and that touch was not lost with the units on either flank.

A battery of field artillery had been detailed to support the advance of this battalion; the forward observation officer went forward with the infantry; the battery, less one section temporarily left behind, moved forward close behind us to a previously selected position from which the Deir Ballut Ridge would be within easy range. A section of machine gunners moved forward close behind the leading companies. In a fold of the ground, some 1,400 yards short of the first objective, the infantry shook out into lines of skirmishers. They continued their advance, and occupied the knoll which was their first objective without opposition.

Meanwhile, after a concentrated bombardment on the left, the first and second of the enemy's forward posts were captured without serious opposition; it appeared probable that these had been occupied mainly for observation and that his principal resistance was to be offered upon the Ballut Ridge.

After a short halt on the first objective, to conform to the timetable, we moved forward again in the same formation against our second objective, a ridge which seemed to overlook the Wadi Deir Ballut. We still met with no opposition, until we put our heads up over the ridge, when we were greeted with a torrent of bullets from machine guns posted on the opposite side of the *wadi*. This *wadi*, it will be remembered, was to us *terra incognita*. The first thing to be done therefore was to make a hurried reconnaissance, and decide on the best method of getting down and across. It was found that the descent was almost a sheer precipice, and that we had not one but two *wadis* to cross; a smaller tributary *wadi*, scarcely marked on the map, forming, in fact, a rather serious obstacle.

Carrying out such a reconnaissance, upon a forward slope, under machine gun fire from across the *wadi*, was none too easy. It had been intended that the leading company, which took the ridge, should at once open covering fire across the *wadi*, whilst the company following should pass through them and cross the *wadi* under cover of their fire. However, the difficulty of taking up suitable positions for seeing the target, and the extremity of the range (about 1,500 yards), made it inadvisable for the infantry to fire. But the machine gunners attached to us soon brought their machine guns into action, while our artillery f.o.o. took up a position on the ridge from which he could fire his guns to good effect.

About this time, away to our left, developed the attack on Mejdel Yaba. This village occupies a commanding position overlooking the plain, and, in Crusading days, was a fortress. That phase of the battle proved an artillery action pure and simple. The whole artillery of a division, with several heavies added, was concentrated on that luck-less spot. It afforded a spectacle not soon to be forgotten. When the infantry arrived, they found the work all over; the Turks had all been killed by the bombardment or fled from the village, most of the latter having been cut off and killed by our machine guns. Before leaving, the Turks had taken the precaution of interviewing the headman of the village and cutting his throat.

To return to our own corner of the picture, under cover of the fire of our own artillery and machine guns the first company went for-ward. Slipping down that mountain side was a veritable case of run-ning the gauntlet. But, once the bottom of the first *wadi* was reached, some cover was afforded for a breather. Almost in front of us, on the far ridge, lay the village of Deir Ballut, on which the enemy evidently intended to base their strongest resistance. On our left, the infantry were making a good pace; on the right they were held up, but, seeing us going forward, they pushed forward too, so that pressure might be maintained all along the line. The enemy had organized his defences and placed his machine guns with great skill.

The slopes of the *wadi* were too steep for good shooting straight down the slope. So he had taken full advantage of the curves and hair-pin bends of the *wadi* to place his machine guns in position sweeping the spurs and giving each other mutual support. Our leading company lost no time in getting to work. They dumped their packs and set out at once to storm the ridge. Meanwhile, our infantry advancing on the left, had taken some of the enemy machine guns in flank, forc-ing them to withdraw, which materially assisted the advance of the leading company. And so the leading company, closely followed by companies in support, established itself on the ridge.

The fiercest of the fighting, however, was yet to come. A great burst of machine-gun fire caused the leading platoon to take cover under one of the terraces. Hence they were at once led forward again. The Turks now delivered a strong counter-attack. Seeing this, the leading platoon dashed forward with their bayonets, led by the company cook, and the Turks were put to flight. The Lewis-gunners caught them as they were getting away and effectually quenched all desire to renew the counter-attack. Then the company pushed forward, and, ignoring the village of Deir Ballut, with its machine guns tried to get across the line of retreat from the village.

Seeing this, the Turks evacuated Deir Ballut, and, under cover of machine guns posted on the further ridges, those left alive made good their escape. That evening found us in undisputed possession of Deir Ballut Ridge from beyond the village of Deir Ballut down to the plain at Mejdel Yaba.

CHAPTER 15

The Mountains of Ephraim

We now found ourselves well established in the Mountains of Ephraim, and at no great distance from the enemy. After the taking of Ballut Ridge he had dropped back, and was soon seen to be entrenching and *sangaring* a new line from 2,000 to 4,000 yards further north. Ballut Ridge had been fixed as our final objective. Had there been possible roads by which guns and supplies could have been brought forward, an immediate pursuit or attack of the enemy might have proved successful; but, with such hopeless communications, deliberate action was a necessity.

After the Ridge had been captured, the enemy were pursued with all the fire from rifles, machine guns and artillery that could be brought to bear. Cavalry, or even infantry pursuit across these mountains was out of the question. An outpost line was established and the troops settled down to a wet and somewhat cheerless night. The mountain sides had been so steep that it had been impossible to bring up any comforts, and even the camels bearing the reserve supply of ammunition could only be got forward with extreme difficulty. Except for shelling, we were left unmolested during the night and next morning, which gave us the opportunity of constructing *sangars*, making tracks for the pack transport animals, and generally making ourselves more comfortable. Patrols were sent forward, and it was ascertained that the country to our immediate front was clear of the enemy.

The effect of this advance was to draw down reinforcements into this sector, and to divert into Palestine reserves of Turkish troops; these came largely from the Caucasus, where the total collapse of Russia had set many good Turkish troops at liberty. There was evidence that these troops had been intended for an offensive campaign in Mesopotamia. It is probable, therefore, that this advance, indirectly, yet substantially, contributed to the defence of Mesopotamia, for the Turkish offensive in that area never materialized. Two or three German divisions came down to stiffen up the Turks, and from this time forward the resistance which we had to face became unmistakeably hardened. The days of campaigning *de luxe* had gone forever. Before our "archies" could get forward, the Hun aeroplanes had very much their own way, and, flying low, dropped bombs and machine-gunned us in a manner that was most uncomfortable.

Enemy artillery shelled any movements on the forward slope, and brought a searching fire to bear, in the hope of damaging our bivouac areas behind the crest. The manner in which the front line was held in the mountains by the Turks as well as by ourselves, was as follows. Strong *sangars* were constituted on the forward slope of a hill or ridge. By day these were occupied only by a small and well-protected observation party, at times supplemented with a Lewis gun team; and the remainder of the garrison were withdrawn behind the crest to bivouac areas on the reverse slope. At dusk, the garrison moved forward and manned the front line, being withdrawn again during the half-light of dawn. Thus the hostile artillery could never see a target upon which to fire. Searching a steep reverse slope with guns is almost impossible while, even with howitzers, unless observation can be obtained, an enormous amount of ammunition has to be fired to secure any result.

Meanwhile, preparations proceeded apace. With a genius little short of that which has made roads across the Himalayas and the Alps, roads were soon engineered down and up the steep sides of the *wadi*, so that within two or three weeks it was possible to bring guns across the *wadi* and over the Ballut Ridge. Water supplies, of which excellent springs were discovered in the bed of the *wadi*, were developed; later, the cisterns on the hills were closed down to prevent mosquito breeding and malaria.

On the 14th March, the enemy moved forward to counter-attack the Ballut Ridge line, but were caught in close formation by our artillery and the counter-attack never developed. On the 19th, a slight advance was made on our right, which brought the village of Beit Rima (possibly the Ramathaim of the Maccabees) within our line. Another forward move was evidently in the wind and patrolling activity increased all along our line.

A detailed account of one of these patrol incidents may be instructive as affording an example of how such a patrol should be handled.

The patrol commander was an experienced soldier who had seen service with almost every battalion of the regiment and in most of the theatres of this war; his sleeve was covered with wound stripes, and hostile snipers only made him angry.

The orders which he received were to patrol as far as Ikba, and to protect some senior officers, who wished to make a reconnaissance and for whose safety he was responsible. He had under his command one platoon, consisting of three sections of riflemen and one of Lewis gunners; also one other officer to assist.

A glance at the sketch map will show Ballut Ridge, which formed our front line, and Three Bushes Hill, the most forward position held by the enemy. Ikba, or to give it its full name, Khurbet Umm el Ikba, thus lay in No Man's Land at no great distance from the enemy. Though standing on a hill and commanding an admirable view of the surrounding country, it is overlooked at a range of a mile from Three Bushes Hill, and also at shorter distances within effective rifle range from the points marked A, B and C, and, to some extent, from the point marked E. F is a lower knoll, commanded from Ikba. Both E and F are commanded from A.

Moving forward before dawn, the patrol commander led his patrol forward down the Wadi Ikba. Each section was kept apart, and moved forward in single file under its own commander. To each section commander were given precise orders as to the position which he was to occupy, what he was to do, and when he was to withdraw. One section moved down the ridge on the right of the *wadi*, and took up a position at the point B. One section, with the junior officer, moved first along the *wadi* bed, and then, while it was still only half light, ascended the left-hand spur and took up a position at A. The Lewis-gun team occupied the hill at C. The remaining section, which had been kept in reserve at the hills about D, now moved forward and occupied Ikba. All being reported clear, the senior officers moved forward, arriving at Ikba just as the daylight became strong enough for them to obtain the forward view of the enemy country which they desired.

An even better view of the country seemed probable from the spur at A. So across there went the officers, including the patrol commander. By the time they arrived, rifle reports were cracking, and the situation was becoming interesting. The reconnaissance finished, the patrol commander gave the senior officers five minutes in which to withdraw, before the expiration of which he would not begin to withdraw his patrol.

Meanwhile, the enemy upon Three Bushes Hill, had espied the party in Ikba, and set out to capture the patrol. Creeping along under cover, they established themselves at the point E. Thence they started to move on to the point F, but came under fire from the section on point A. It became a case of running the gauntlet, but the section were shooting well and dropped their men. The section at Ikba was withdrawing; the enemy, failing to realize that the spur A was occupied, rushed across to A intending to shoot up the *wadi* at the section withdrawing from Ikba. They were greeted with a warm reception from the section already at A and beat a hasty retreat.

The section at A now withdrew up the *wadi*, covered by the fire of the section still in position at B and by the Lewis gunners at C. The reserve section from Ikba, who had been the first to withdraw, had meanwhile taken up another section in rear, and, under their protection, the section at B and the Lewis-gunners from C withdrew up the *wadi*. The enemy had apparently had enough of it, for the pursuit was not pressed. A few rounds of shrapnel were fired at us as a parting present, but no casualties were sustained.

This patrol commander had paid attention to, and illustrated the soundness of, the cardinal principles of mountain fighting, namely, the necessity for seizing and piquetting the commanding heights, and the support of the movement of one party of troops by the fire of other parties already in position. The plan of using the Lewis gun as a reserve of fire, kept well back to cover the retirement of the remainder, was undoubtedly sound. Had the commanding heights not been first secured, it is difficult to see how the patrol could have withdrawn in the face of the enemy without confusion and without casualty.

On the 27th March the whole line moved forward. The advance was only intended to be for a depth of about a mile, in order to secure a better tactical line for defence. None of the objectives were believed to be held by the enemy. Accordingly, the advance was carried out by night. A full moon, giving light throughout the night, facilitated the operation. As soon as daylight was gone, the whole line crept noiselessly forward, with bayonets fixed ready to meet any possible opposition with cold steel. Away to our right, the enemy detected movement, and put down a barrage. But their firing was somewhat wild; the barrage came down behind the advancing troops and caused no casualties.

On our front the enemy had not awakened to what was taking place, and our objectives were attained without molestation. It was realized that our new positions would be overlooked from the enemy's observation posts on Three Bushes Hill and on Arara, and that, when they saw us by daylight occupying the nearer ridges, they would shell us unmercifully. Accordingly, the remainder of the night was not devoted to sleep, but to the intensive building of *sangars* on the new defensive line, and the preparations of bivouac areas in such few spots as might be under cover from view and from fire. When morning came, the enemy commenced to shell, but the night had not been wasted, and our fellows had made themselves secure.

This new line was not very comfortable. To such an extent was it overlooked by the enemy that all movement by day was out of the question, and even incinerator fires had for a time to be forbidden. The enemy attacked this new line a few days after it had been taken up. However, our artillery caught the enemy's troops in close order before they had been deployed, and so we experienced no greater inconvenience than a bombardment, doing no great damage. It was not expected that this new line would have to be held for any great length of time. Already preparations were being pushed on for another encounter with the enemy.

CHAPTER 16

Rafat

We have seen, in an earlier chapter, that throughout the campaign in Palestine the left British flank, near the sea, was at all times much in advance of the right. We have already discussed the cause and advantages; there was one distinct disadvantage. As the trend of the country sloped up from the Maritime Plain, the enemy on our right front was on higher ground and had the advantages of observation. If there were a commanding position to our front, and we moved forward and captured it, we found that there were yet other positions beyond, from which that position was itself commanded. Our positions on the Ephraim Mountains along the Ballut Ridge were at this time overlooked from three commanding hills in the possession of the enemy, known as Arara, Rafat, and Three Bushes. Further to the right were the villages of El Kep and Berukin, also on high ground. Owing to the conformation of the country the key of this district was Arara.

In order to improve the general line, and in preparation for a further advance, it was decided to move forward and to capture all these commanding positions. Accordingly, on the morning of the 9th April, the line moved forward. The village of El Kep was a nest of machine guns. After heavy bombardment it was captured after stubborn resistance. Berukin was also captured after sharp fighting, but further progress in this locality was held up. Next day these villages were heavily counter-attacked, and, though they were firmly held, further progress was out of the question.

Meanwhile, a battalion of Somersets had captured Rafat, and a battalion of Dorsets Three Bushes Hill. Enemy shelling now became intense, followed up by counter-attacks, all of which were repulsed.

The intention had been that the Somersets should capture Rafat first and then take Arara, the main objective of these operations. The capture of Three Bushes Hill was necessary to secure Arara and Rafat from reverse fire. But, to enable Arara to be held, it was also necessary to capture other heights to the south-east, notably one called The Pimple. Most of these heights were captured, but, although determined efforts were made, the enemy could not be dislodged from The Pimple. Nevertheless, the Somersets moved forward from Rafat and successfully established themselves upon Arara. Here they were fired at from all sides.

They found that Arara was itself commanded from a height called Sheikh Silbih, a thousand or two yards beyond, while the reserve fire from the machine guns on The Pimple soon made their position on Arara untenable. They fell back upon, and firmly established themselves in, their positions at Rafat. One lad, who was left behind in this retirement, had a terrible experience. Wounded in three or four places, he was unable to withdraw with the remainder of his company. He lay out on Arara for three days, after which he was discovered by some Turks. These proceeded to strip him, whereupon he made known to them that he was still alive. They then bayonetted him, and left him for dead. He lay out there for yet another day, now naked, when he was found by a German stretcher-party. These took pity upon him, and removed him to a hospital where he was nursed back to life.

The position on Three Bushes Hill had become interesting. If left in our undisputed possession, it would have rendered the main line of enemy trenches untenable. On the other hand, if the enemy could drive us off, he might from there roll up Rafat and our other positions. He therefore made several determined attempts throughout the day to retake this hill. The position was not altogether unlike that on Spion Kop. Each side clung to the slope immediately below the summit, the forward slope being untenable through shell fire; our guns were unable to silence the hostile batteries. There was this difference, however, from Spion Kop, for here there was no question at present of withdrawing.

The difficulties of bringing supplies, water and ammunition up, and the even greater difficulty of carrying the wounded down a pathless precipice 400 feet high, can be better imagined than described. This work had mostly to be done by night, for our communication line was under enemy observation. The last of the ambulance camels, which were evacuating wounded from the regimental aid post had not crossed the Ballut Ridge and got out of sight before dawn, and were shelled accordingly.

The enemy delivered counter-attacks again in the night; these also were repulsed. Next morning he changed his tactics. Continuing to shell the back areas, he now pushed up snipers, who established themselves where they could fire at any movement. In so far as the snipers near the summit of the ridge were concerned, a service of counter-sniping was established. But, what was more difficult to deal with, he established snipers on the lower slopes of his own side of the ridge, who could look down upon, and make themselves unpleasant towards, Rafat. Accordingly, it was decided to clear the forward slope.

The Dorsets had now been fighting on the hill for forty-eight hours. Accordingly, on the night of the 10th/11th, they were relieved by an Indian battalion, the Outrans. Just before dawn this battalion moved forward, surprised the Turks, drove them down the hill and consolidated a line along the forward slope, with observation posts and Lewis gunners, withdrawing the remainder of the battalion behind the crest.

The sniping had thus been stopped for the time, and the day was passed in comparative quiet. At dusk, that evening, down came one of the most furious bombardments put down by the enemy in Palestine. Guns from all quarters concentrated on the hill, and practically blotted out the devoted band that were holding the forward line. The bombardment was followed up by a determined counter-attack, but this was repulsed, the battalion of Dorsets being brought back to support the Outrans on the hill.

It was now realized that the only way by which the Arara position could be captured and held, was by a general advance of the line to at least a thousand yards farther to the north, so as to capture The Pimple, Sheikh Subih, and the enemy works beyond Three Bushes. Accordingly, preparations were put in hand, and all was ready for this further advance, when there came—the disaster in France.

The great German offensive in France had commenced on the 21st March, and, a few days later, occurred that great break through which very nearly altered the whole complexion of the war. At first this was not allowed to prejudice the operations in Palestine. But, as the seriousness of the situation in France became realized, no effort was spared to collect more men to fill the gap. Orders were given to cease all further active operations on a large scale in Palestine, and to send to France all the men that could be spared.

Accordingly, there was no alternative but to consolidate, to heavily wire and sangar in upon the line that had been already reached, making such tactical readjustments as were necessary.

It might appear at first sight that the net result of these operations was negative, and that the poor fellows who had given their lives here had died in vain. But this was not so. Rafat was destined to become famous. It was fortified on an almost impregnable scale, thousands of pounds were spent, and a couple of million sand-bags were worked into its defences. A veritable fortress was established which overlooked much of the enemy positions. More than once was this fortress attacked by the Turks, but in vain. It ultimately formed the firm pivot on which was based the great sweep which conquered Palestine.

Feeling between the Turks and the Germans was growing intensely bitter. Germans were not allowed to walk about singly behind the Turkish lines, for fear of assassination. In an attack made by them in the Jordan Valley in July, not only did the Turks fail to move forward in support of the Germans, but they actually fired upon the Germans, when, through lack of that support, they were compelled to retire. It was a case of "a house divided against itself" and it could not therefore hope long to stand.

Active operations on a large scale in Palestine having been stopped, the army was not reorganized. It was a matter of keen regret to many who had followed the fortunes of this campaign since the days of Gaza, that they and their battalions were not to play a part in the final act. The 52nd and the 74th Divisions were withdrawn entirely, their places being taken by the 3rd and 7th Indian Divisions from Mesopotamia. All those remaining, except the 54th, were converted into Indian Divisions, 75 *per cent* of their battalions being withdrawn and replaced by fresh battalions from India. Those withdrawn were, in some cases, sent to France, in others, broken up and used for reinforcements in the country. Hitherto the army in Palestine had consisted mainly of Territorials. Henceforth it was to consist mainly of Indians.

Chapter 17

The Crowning Victory

The Turkish forces in Palestine, in the autumn of 1918, consisted of three armies, the 8th and the 7th, plus one added division on the west of the Jordan, and the 4th army on the east. All were under the supreme command of the German General, Liman von Sanders.

The line held by the enemy west of the Jordan extended roughly from the sea, south of the Nahr ek Falyk (some 14 miles north of Jaffa), across western Palestine approximately east, south-east to near Rafat, thence easterly and south-easterly, across the Nablus-Jerusalem Road, and so down to the Jordan Valley. Thus, a portion of his force was entrenched across the Maritime Plain, while the remainder was in the mountains of the Central Range. These mountains of Ephraim and Samaria form a rugged, isolated plateau, which is bounded on the north and east by the low-lying Valleys of Esdraelon and the Jordan. North-west, the mountains continue in a broken chain, till they fall precipitously to the sea at Cape Carmel.

There were two or three routes available to the enemy for supply or retreat, behind the Samaritan plateau. Most important of these was the railway, which, leaving the main Damascus-Hejaz line at Deraa, ran westwards down the Yarmuk Valley to the Jordan, thence through Beisan, and up the Vale of Jezreel and along the Plain of Esdraelon to Haifa. From El Afule, a junction in the middle of the Esdraelon Plain, the south-bound line branched off, and, passing through Jenin (close by Jezreel), wound its way among the mountains up to Messudieh Station, close to Samaria. Thence a short line ran on to Nablus, while the main line continued down the slope of the Wadi Shair to the Maritime Plain, which it reached at Tul Keram.

The advanced enemy bases at Nablus and Tul Keram were served also by good roads. That from Tul Keram followed the line of the railway up to a point near Samaria, where it joined the main north-bound road leading from Nablus down to Jenin and El Afule. From El Afule it would be possible to go down the Vale of Jezreel (along the road where Jehu drove furiously) to Beisan, and thence northward up the Jordan Valley. But the better road from Jenin and El Afule leads across the Plain of Esdraelon to Nazareth and Tiberias and round the northern side of the Sea of Galilee to Damascus. Another road from Nablus leads eastwards, and, dropping steeply down along the Wadi Fara, leads to the Jordan, which it crosses by a ford at Jisr ed Damie. The places of tactical importance on the enemy lines of communication behind his advanced bases were, therefore, the railway junctions at Deraa and El Afule, the ford of Jisr ed Damie, and the towns of Beisan, Jenin and Nazareth.

The broad outline of General Allenby's plan of operations was an attack in overwhelming force against the enemy's positions on the Maritime Plain, followed by a right wheel of his left flank on a front of 16 miles from Rafat to the sea, thereby rolling up the Turkish line and driving them all into the Samaritan hills; meanwhile, his cavalry were to dash for the tactical points behind the Turkish line and so close all enemy lines of retreat.

Some weeks before the date fixed for the commencement of operations, the several divisions were by turn withdrawn behind the line and put through a three weeks' course of intensive training. Then a rearrangement of the line took place, whereby an overwhelming force was concentrated on the left. The 60th Division, and most of the cavalry, were moved across to the extreme left from the Jordan Valley. Divisions in the line were so rearranged that the line from Rafat to the right was only held thinly, while the garrison of the line from Rafat to the sea was doubled by the addition of three more divisions, including the 60th on the sea and a French division at Rafat.

All these movements were carried out with the utmost secrecy. The fact that the push was coming along the Maritime Plain was successfully camouflaged, and the enemy led to believe that the push would come up the Jordan Valley. The hotel at Jerusalem was closed, and got in readiness, ostensibly for occupation by G.H.Q. Empty lorries were run up and down the Jordan Valley. Tents were left standing there and dummy-horse lines arranged. Dummy horses were left in the Jordan Valley to convey to enemy aerial observers the impression that cavalry were still there in strength.

All the marching towards the Jordan Valley was by day; all the marching towards the Maritime Plain was carried out by night, while by day these troops were hidden in the olive and orange groves that abound on this portion of the plain. So successful were these ruses, and so complete the surprise, that enemy aerial reconnaissances, made a day before the attack, reported that there was unusual movement in the Jordan Valley and that there was no unusual movement on the coastal sector. The whole of the operations were a triumph of secrecy and of organization.

On the day before the main attack, a small advance was carried out by the right wing just west of the Jordan, occupying El Mugheir. This place is the junction of several roads leading from the west to the east of the Jordan. The object of this preliminary move was to prevent the Turks west of the river escaping by this route to the east, and also to draw the attention of the enemy towards the Jordan Valley and distract it from the coastal sector.

By the night of the 18th/19th September, our troops were in position. The divisions occupying the line from the sea on the left were the 60th, the 7th and the 75th on the Plain, the 3rd where plain and hills meet about Mejdel Yaba, the 54th and the French at Rafat. Thence the line was held by the 10th Division, assisted by a composite force, and, on the extreme right, about the recently captured Mugheir, by the 53rd. Cavalry were concentrated behind the 60th Division ready to dash forward directly the line should be broken.

At 4.30 on the morning of the 19th September, there suddenly opened an intensive bombardment of the enemy's coastal positions, carried out by all the artillery, trench-mortars and machine-guns that could be concentrated in this small sector, the navy also co-operating. After ten minutes' bombardment, the infantry moved forward and assaulted the enemy's front line positions, which were carried with but little opposition. Thereafter the barrage lifted and crept, being supplemented in places by smoke barrages dropped from aeroplanes. The infantry pushed forward and captured the enemy's second and third lines and strong points in rear.

Shortly before seven o'clock, the 60th Division had broken right through the enemy defences by the sea, and had reached, and established a bridge-head at the Wadi Nahr el Falyk, a mile or so behind the enemy line. Engineers and pioneers got to work at once, and in a very short space of time had made roads and bridges through the enemy trench system, and over the Nahr el Falyk, by which cavalry and guns could be pushed forward. At 7.30, the cavalry passed through on their dash for the tactical points behind the enemy's lines.

Meanwhile, all along the line our infantry had taken their first objectives with little opposition, the enemy having been taken completely by surprise. The whole line advanced to a maximum depth of 5 miles, and then swung to the right, pivoting on Rafat. Such opposition as was encountered was met with at the strong points well behind the front line, where the enemy had had the time and opportunity to man his defences. For example, both at El Tireh and at Kalkilieh, stubborn resistance was encountered. Thus the line swung right-handed into the hills, crumpling up the whole enemy line west of Rafat. The 60th Division, after their break through, marched for the greater part of the day, and, by 5.30 in the afternoon, had reached Tul Keram. Our line, that evening, ran approximately south and north from Rafat to Tul Keram.

The cavalry passing through the gaps broken at the sea and close to Tabsor, pushed rapidly northward along the Coastal Plain. Some of them made for Tul Keram, and, passing thence up the Valley towards Nablus, had already reached Anebta before dark, cutting off large bodies of the retreating enemy with guns and transport between Tul Keram and the railway junction at Messudieh. Another strong cavalry force moved farther north. They passed through the mountains east of Mount Carmel that night, by the Musmus Pass (Megiddo), and, early on the following morning, the 20th, they charged the enemy holding the northern exit of the pass and debouched on to the Plain of Esdraelon (Armageddon).

These seized the railway junction at El Afule. Some pushed on eastwards towards the Jordan and captured Beisan (Bethshan), some northwards and captured Nazareth, while some, turning southwards, took Jenin in reverse. By nightfall on the 20th all these tactical points were in our possession.

Yet another exploit remains to be chronicled. Far away across the eastern desert, but beautifully co-ordinated, and working as part of one great machine, moved a raiding force of the Arab troops of Hussein, King of the Hejaz. At the critical moment these swooped down upon the junction at Deraa, where they destroyed the railway in all directions, completely depriving the enemy of their main line of retirement.

Throughout the operations our airmen had the time of their lives. Some hovered all day over the enemy aerodrome at Jenin, and effectually prevented enemy machines from leaving the ground. Some maintained contact between the infantry and the higher command. Some, flying low, bombed and machine-gunned the retreating Turks, and completed their confusion.

The advance was continued on the 20th. On this day, the 10th Division, which had hitherto remained stationary to the right of Rafat, moved forward in a north-easterly direction, taking in rear the strong enemy position at Furkha. The whole line was now advancing and driving the retreating Turks towards Samaria and Nablus, and down the roads leading northwards and eastwards from these points. By the evening of the 20th, the Turkish resistance had collapsed everywhere on the west of the Jordan, except on the Turkish left in the Jordan Valley. Our right wing had advanced slightly, and occupied a line from near El Mugheir to Es Sawieh, while our left wing had swung round and reached the line Bidich-Baka-Messudieh Junction—that is to say, we were gradually closing in on Nablus from the south, south-west, and west. Owing to the tactical positions behind the enemy lines having been seized by our cavalry, all avenues of escape which might have been open to the enemy had been closed, except the fords across the Jordan between Beisan and Jisr-ed-Damieh.

By the 21st, the retreating Turks had become a demoralized rabble, fleeing to the fords of the Jordan, like the discomfited Midianites, under Oreb and Zeeb, had fled more than three thousand years before from the pursuit of Gideon. Those who fled down the northward road were captured and collected by our cavalry at Jenin. Those who fled down the eastward road by the Wadi Fara, hoping to reach the still open ford at Jisr-ed-Damieh, met with a more cruel fate. This road led down a steep and narrow gorge, dominated by the heights east of Nablus. A brigade of the 10th Division was rushed forward by a forced march, and seized these heights, effectually closing the trap.

Our airmen had already got the situation well in hand here, and the road soon became a veritable shambles. The enemy had been forced or shepherded by our infantry into this bottle-neck, and our airmen, swooping down to 200 feet and bombing the head of the column, soon made the road impassable. That accomplished, they flew up and down the struggling column, bombing and machine-gunning without let or hindrance. It seemed as though the unspeakable Turk had at last been delivered over to vengeance in this Valley of Death. An eye-witness[1] describes the scene.

---

1. Mr. W. T. Massey, Official Correspondent with the E.E.F.

In no section of Napoleon's retreat from Moscow could there have been a more terrible picture of hopeless and irretrievable defeat. In this area alone, eighty-seven guns of various calibres, and fully a thousand horse and oxen-drawn vehicles, nearly a hundred motor-lorries, cars, field-kitchens, water carts, and a mass of other impedimenta blocked the road, with the carcases of thousands of animals and the bodies of dead Turks and Germans.

On the 22nd, our cavalry moved up the Jordan Valley and seized the ford at Jisr-ed-Damieh, thus cutting off the last possible means of escape. Prisoners were surrendering in thousands. They looked weak and exhausted; in many cases they had fled over a parched country and beneath a burning sun for three or four days, without touching a drop of water. Their plight was pitiable. By that evening, the Turkish armies west of the Jordan had ceased to exist.

There still remained the Turkish 4th army in Eastern Palestine. An expedition, consisting largely of cavalry, was sent against them. These crossed the Jordan Valley, and, moving up the eastern slopes, on the 23rd September captured Es Salt, and, on the 26th, Amman. A day or two later, the Turkish force south of Amman, about 10,000 strong, surrendered. The remainder of the Turkish 4th army tried to withdraw. They were closely pursued by our cavalry and airmen, and, to some extent, cut off by the Arab forces of the King of the Hejaz. Many prisoners were taken from this army, while, such as could do so, made their escape to Damascus.

The whole of Palestine, south of, and including the Plain of Esdraelon, was now in the hands of the British and their Arab allies. But there was still work to be done in a sweep forward towards Damascus. The Turks had some reserves at Damascus, and with these, and the remnants of their 4th army, they attempted to check our advance against that city. Accordingly, they sent a small force down to the Upper Jordan, that is, to the river north of the Sea of Galilee. This force, which consisted of Germans, Turks and Circassians, was rushed down from Damascus in motor-lorries, in order to deny the crossing at Jisr Benat Yakub. They blew up the bridge and covered the crossing with machine guns. On the 27th our cavalry, pushing north from Tiberias, swam the river both to the south and to the north of this crossing, and surprised and captured many of the enemy. They then, with armoured cars, pushed forward along the main Tiberias-Damascus road.

On the same day, other cavalry joined hands with the Arab army at Deraa. From this point, also, cavalry and armoured cars pushed northward. It seemed a question whether this force or that from Jisr Benat Yakub would be the first to reach Damascus, as both forces were rapidly approaching the city from the south and south-west respectively. The advance was still disputed by enemy rear guards, from whom prisoners and guns were captured. The enemy rearguards were defeated, and, by the evening of the 30th, the city was partially surrounded.

Early on the morning of the 1st October, a British force and a portion of the Arab army of King Hussein occupied the city of Damascus.

In the course of a fortnight the enemy line had been broken; Samaria, Galilee, Eastern Palestine and Damascus had been conquered; three Turkish armies had been destroyed, with a loss of their entire war material; and over 350 guns and 71,000 prisoners had been captured.

CHAPTER 18

Conclusion

Serious fighting had practically finished with the capture of Damascus. The northward flight of the Turks continued, closely pursued by our cavalry and armoured cars. A division of infantry was brought forward in support, but the difficulties of supplying a large force so far away from a base made it impossible to bring forward the infantry in any strength. Australians rounded up a Turkish column some miles north of Damascus, and a few thousand more prisoners were captured. Beyrout, the port of Damascus, was abandoned without a blow, and, on the 6th October, was occupied by the allies. A division of French troops was landed here, and, thereafter, this port became the main channel of supply for the troops operating in Northern Syria.

Our forces pushed on northwards, meeting with little or no opposition, and occupying Baalbek, Tripolis and Homs. A Turkish force, under General Liman von Sanders, and estimated at about 12,000, concentrated a few miles south of Aleppo, where they threatened to offer some resistance. The advance northward was, however, unopposed. The enemy had constructed trenches covering Aleppo, and at first showed signs of holding them. But, after our armoured cars had got into touch, and our airmen had bombed them, the enemy decided to evacuate, and withdrew to the hills towards Alexandretta. Aleppo was entered by our cavalry on the 26th October, and the station was seized at Muslimie, the junction of the Baghdad Railway. By these captures we had made ourselves masters of the main line of communications with Constantinople of the Turkish armies in Mesopotamia.

Their armies virtually destroyed, the Turks now concluded an armistice, which took effect as from the 31st October. Their allies, the Bulgarians, who had suffered disastrous reverses in Macedonia, had just concluded an armistice; the Austrians were being badly beaten by the Italians and were clearly nearing the end; and the Germans were fast retiring from France and Belgium: so, with all hope of succour gone, the Turks had no alternative but to conclude an armistice, the terms of which practically amounted to unconditional surrender.

The terms of the armistice included the following. Immediate demobilization of the Turkish Army, except troops required for the surveillance of the frontier and the maintenance of internal order; the surrender of the garrisons of the Hejaz, Assir, Yemen, Syria and Mesopotamia, and the withdrawal of troops from Cilicia; the surrender of all ports there; occupation by the Allies of the Taurus Mountains tunnel system; the allied control of all railways; occupation by the Allies of any strategic points considered necessary for their security; prohibition of destruction of military or similar material; all Germans and Austrians to quit Turkey within a month; Turkey to cease all relations with the Central Powers; all allied prisoners in Turkish possession to be handed over unconditionally, but Turkish prisoners in the Allies' hands to be kept at the disposal of the Allies. In addition, all war vessels in Turkish waters were to be surrendered, the Dardanelles were to be opened, and free access secured for allied ships to all Turkish ports and exchanges and to the Black Sea.

A few days later, Austria threw in her hand, and, on the 11th November, an armistice was concluded with Germany. The Central Powers had surrendered. The greatest war in the history of the world had been brought to a close.

Will our campaign be passed down to history as "The Last Crusade"? Presumably not. Throughout the campaign there was little or no religious animosity, except that the Moslem Turk extended no quarter to the Hindoo. To speak of this as a campaign of The Cross against The Crescent is untrue. The Turkish high command was controlled by Germans, so-called Christians. The British soldier fought with no less zest than when opposed to Turks. At the final battle, the Moslems, serving in our armies, by far outnumbered the Christians.

The close of the great war forms a fitting point at which to bring our story also to a close. Its aim has been a blend of history and reminiscence. Much has been set down here which would have been omitted from a history; much more has been omitted which a complete history would have contained. In particular I plead guilty to omitting names of units deserving of special mention. Generally their names have not been known to me; in such cases as they were known, I have feared that to mention them might have caused more jealousy than satisfaction. We each of us think, and rightly so, that our own unit does better than any other engaged. So, many a reader may be disappointed at finding no mention of the unit in which he is particularly interested. I can only refer him to the congratulatory telegrams which his unit received in the field, and which are doubtless preserved among the records of the regiment.

We have now completed our brief review of this campaign. We have seen its small beginnings in the defence of the Suez Canal, when Turkey, leaning upon Germany, a broken reed, vaunted herself in an attempt to conquer Egypt. We have traced the footsteps of the British Army as, pushing back the invading Turk, it crept across the desert. We have watched its struggles on the frontier of Asia, culminating in the victory of Gaza and Beersheba. We have followed its progress in the onward sweep, which conquered Jerusalem, and watched it through succeeding months of trial, patience and disappointment. Finally, we have seen it destroy the remnants of the Turkish armies, and, in one great rush, conquer the whole of Northern Syria. Proud, indeed, should those of us feel who have been privileged to play a part in this campaign.

www.ingramcontent.com/pod-product-compliance
Lightning Source LLC
Chambersburg PA
CBHW021010090426
42738CB00007B/738